Norman Maccoll, Norman Maccoll

The Greek Sceptics from Pyrrho to Sextus

an essay which obtained the Hare prize in the year 1868

Norman Maccoll, Norman Maccoll

The Greek Sceptics from Pyrrho to Sextus
an essay which obtained the Hare prize in the year 1868

ISBN/EAN: 9783742800770

Manufactured in Europe, USA, Canada, Australia, Japa

Cover: Foto ©Andreas Hilbeck / pixelio.de

Manufactured and distributed by brebook publishing software (www.brebook.com)

Norman Maccoll, Norman Maccoll

The Greek Sceptics from Pyrrho to Sextus

THE GREEK SCEPTICS.

THE GREEK SCEPTICS,

FROM

PYRRHO TO SEXTUS.

An Essay
WHICH OBTAINED THE HARE PRIZE IN THE YEAR 1868.

BY
NORMAN MACCOLL, B.A.,
SCHOLAR OF DOWNING COLLEGE, CAMBRIDGE.

Ὁ μέντοι Ἀρκεσίλαος πάνυ μοι δοκεῖ Πυρρωνείοις κοινωνεῖν λόγοις, ὡς μίαν εἶναι σχεδὸν τὴν κατ' αὐτὸν ἀγωγὴν καὶ τὴν ἡμετέραν.
SEXT. EMP. *P. H.* I. 232.

PATRI MEO.

For the following essay I have consulted more or less constantly the lectures of Hegel and the histories of philosophy by Tennemann, Ritter, Brandis, Schwegler and Erdmann, and the history of Logic by Prof. Prantl. I am more particularly indebted to the history of Zeller, and for bibliographical notices, to the manual of Ueberweg. I have used a paper on Aenesidemus by the late M. Saisset, in his work called "Le Scepticisme," a Gymnasium "programm" by Geffers "de Arcesila," and a monograph on the same subject as the present essay, by M. Thorbecke, in the Annals of the University of Leyden. I regret I have had little opportunity of using a paper by Prof. Kayser in the "Rheinisches Museum" on Sextus Empiricus. I have consulted without advantage the history of Scepticism by Stäudlin: that by Tafel I could find neither in the Public Library, nor in the British Museum, nor in the Bibliothèque Impériale.

THE GREEK SCEPTICS.

THE death of Aristotle marks the close of a great epoch in the course of Greek speculation—an epoch which, beginning with the Sophists, includes a term of little more than one hundred years: yet within that brief compass is comprised all that is most brilliant and perfect in ancient philosophy. When it began, Greek thinkers had just emancipated themselves from the cosmological theories current in Ionia nearly two hundred years before: when it closed, the most complete and far-reaching system had been promulgated to which the ancient world ever attained. Whether we look to the wide circle of knowledge embraced, the new methods adopted, or the precision introduced, we cannot but allow that the progress was immense. As Rome, from being a petty state struggling for existence on the Tiber and the slopes of the Apennines, rose in a few score years to be the mistress of all the peoples who dwelt on the shores of the Mediterranean, Greek philosophy, in its infancy a vague and crude attempt to solve the problems, that lie most closely before our eyes, had, by the time of Aristotle, mapped out and to some extent formed the paths, along which all subsequent thinkers have been forced to travel. Xenophanes and Anaxagoras had made only the beginnings of a distinction between the several provinces of thought. Psychology was still unknown: Logic was all but unrecognized as having a claim to a separate existence[1]; it was but dimly perceived that there is a difference between physics and ethics. In Aristotle, on the contrary, we find a scientific method resting largely on observation and experiment, and a scientific terminology of marvellous richness. The boundaries of the sciences are definitely laid down: their relations ascertained; their objects determined, and also to some extent investigated.

In Plato and Aristotle ancient speculation reached its culminating point, and to us at the present day they appear to stand far above all who followed them, and yet it is very noteworthy how slight was the influence they exercised over the thinkers of the three following centuries. Their systems were neither accepted as final, and as rendering unnecessary any further inquiry, except in the way of comment and illustration; nor, on the other hand, were they sharply criticized; their shortcomings pointed out, and new theories formed with the endeavour at least to avoid their supposed errors. They were neither used as models nor warnings. The very faults they are most

[1] Cf. Prantl. *Gesch. d. Logik*, I. pp. 10, 11.

chargeable with—faults, which are in great part the result of imperfect observation and too hasty generalization[1]—were reproduced in an exaggerated form in Zeno and Epicurus. Outside the circle of their professed followers[2], not much quoted, and—Aristotle especially—not much read, they were neglected or, one might rather say, abandoned by an age which had a different tone of thought and a different aim. This was the result of a change that came over not philosophers only, but the intellect and the feelings of all Greece.

That outward circumstances and mental dispositions act and re-act on one another, is a truth that has almost passed into a truism, but in Greece it was a fact pre-eminently true and important. There the tie which bound the citizen to his city was so close, so far closer indeed than such relations are or can be in a modern state, that the fortunes of the city swayed with a power unknown to us the thoughts and feelings of the citizens. With us local prejudices and associations not uncommonly chill or check general patriotism, but to the Greek there was no such imperium in imperio. With him local prejudices and general patriotism were one and the same thing, for his state was his birth-place, and he had no feeling more

[1] Zeller, *Phil. der Gr.* III. a. p. 2.
[2] The strange story regarding the fate of Aristotle's writings, told by Strabo (XIII. 1. 148), and in slightly different terms by Plutarch, may have had its origin in this neglect of Aristotle. On Cicero's ignorance of Aristotle, see Madvig, ad Cic. *de Fin.* IV. 12.

local or more present than love of his country. Her successes gladdened him, her disasters came home to him, without anything interposed to deaden the joy or diminish the sorrow. And for him, his state was all-sufficient. Except when a faint thought of Pan-Hellenism flitted across his mind, it formed a perfect whole, beyond which he neither saw nor aspired. If he wandered from home, he found other states constituted in much the same fashion—monads like his own.

But the generation which listened to Aristotle, was also witness of a great revolution. It felt the first pressure of the foreign rule, which soon crushed the liberties of Hellas. The states of Greece and the colonies in the Ægæan sea became a prize to be struggled for by the generals, who quarrelled over the heritage of Alexander: Magna Græcia was fast waning before the Sabellian and the Latin; and Agathocles and the Carthaginians were alike fatal to the prosperity of the Sicilian Republics. The incessant feuds, which had formerly prevailed between state and state, had been a curse to Greece, yet they had not been without benefit, but the wars of the Diadochi were ruinous to the cities and peoples who were the subjects of contention. Freedom was gone, wealth declined, and the flower of the people wandered away to seek a better fortune in the mercenary armies and half-Hellenic half-Oriental cities of Ptolemy and Seleucus. Everywhere the old life, which the

Greeks had cherished so fondly, and to which they clung with such tenacity, was decaying: the old words, State and Society, which had been so mighty, lost their reality and therefore their influence in the midst of anarchy and misrule, and it seemed mere mockery to suppose that the individual was to be sought in the state, that the state was the individual writ large. How could any one imagine man to be a political being, or fancy that individuals were but incidental parts of the whole body of the state? Who could hope to realize a new scheme of polity, such as Plato perhaps had dreamed of achieving with the help of Dion and Dionysius? What community would now ask a philosopher to draw up its laws[1]? Laws had come to be given by the stater and sarissa. Need we wonder that in such a state of things men turned from the misery without to seek for happiness within? Between them and their fathers lay a gulf as wide as between France of the Old Monarchy and France of the Restoration. Circumstances were so altered that they had neither the same sympathies nor the same longings. Plato and Aristotle failed to satisfy, not from theoretical defects, nor from the contradictions, that lay concealed in their philosophies, but because men wanted, instead of a speculation that could embrace the universe, a help in their need, a doctrine by which

---

[1] Diog. Laërt. III. § 23.

to live. This is the reason why Plato and Aristotle passed out of repute. Like all men of the highest genius they had thought and written not for their own age merely, but for posterity. The feelings and the fashions of their time and country, though they much affected them, yet coloured the vision of their contemporaries far more than their own: they stood above and looked beyond that, which was immediately around and before them. And they had to pay the penalty of genius. Too far before their time to be in sympathy with it, they could not satisfy the needs of a generation, which, much more deeply stirred than their own, was for that very reason much more absorbed by the events and circumstances amidst which it lived and suffered. Men thirsted for a philosophy that would meet the wants which these events had excited, for something that would give the individual that happiness which the outside world could no longer afford; and to this demand all the sects alike endeavoured to frame an answer. If political freedom had departed, still, the Stoics said, the individual might be free—free from responsibility to others, in that he was responsible to himself alone—free from external law, as having a higher law in himself. If the restless activity and ambition, which had been so dear to the Greeks, and to the Athenians especially[1], were now impossible, Epicurus taught that this fretful energy had embittered life, that it must

[1] Thuc. I. c. 70.

and ought to be abandoned for the obedience to nature. When turmoil prevailed without, when might seemed right, the Pyrrhonean extolled that pure apathy of the soul which rises far above the jars of life, which, if it knows no good, yet knows no evil.

In such a state of things speculation in the highest sense ceased to be. It was no longer pursued with a purely scientific aim: it was cultivated not for its own sake, but simply as a means to an end, and, however different the tenets of the different schools, that end was always the same. In this point at least they were at one. Not in their ethics merely, but in every part of their systems, in the Stoic Teleology, in the atomic theories of Epicurus, in the sceptical rejection of all physics, happiness is the keynote. Knowledge is power, but knowledge is also happiness.

"Felix qui potuit rerum cognoscere causas."

The first great advance in philosophy had been made, when from consideration of the object the Sophists had turned to the thinking and willing subject, and had thereby laid the foundations of Psychological Philosophy. "Πάντων χρημάτων," so runs the famous dictum of Protagoras, "μέτρον ἄνθρωπος, τῶν μὲν ὄντων ὡς ἔστι, τῶν δὲ οὐκ ὄντων ὡς οὐκ ἔστι." The principle of subjectivity thus enunciated runs through all subsequent philosophy. We trace it plainly in Plato and Aristotle, but with them, though powerful, it still plays a subordinate rôle. In their successors it was sovereign everywhere. It triumphed in politics when the republican governments decayed: it triumphed in art when sculpture and painting became mere portraiture: philosophy it changed and altered as it chose. There was nothing at home that could dispute its ascendancy, and intercourse with the newly conquered East was as yet too recent to allow of the introduction from abroad of any counteracting elements. The Greek mind was little disposed to the reception of foreign ideas, and it was only by slow degrees and, after all, through the mediation of Jewish thinkers, that it became in some degree impressed by Oriental influences; and this took place not before but after the commencement of the Christian Era.

Philosophy was thus entirely altered in character and direction. It became thoroughly eudæmonistic and thoroughly subjective—for the happiness, that was its aim, was not happiness in the abstract, but happiness in relation to the individual—and it resolved itself into the problem of determining in the first place the nature of this happiness, in the second the means of attaining it. On the former question there was less real difference of opinion between the rival sects than one would perhaps be led to expect. With them all, the highest ideal conceived was a negative one, for they alike abhorred conditions, and agreed in seeking developement for the subject free and independent of any disturbing element. The world around, in its essence changeable and variable, could in any case only disturb and vex the soul: the soul must seek peace and quiet within itself and for itself. Even the so-called cosmopolitanism of the Stoic was but a loosening of the ties that might hinder this self-sufficiency. In such a scheme, Ethics of course grew to be the chief subject of inquiry, a result not a little furthered by the great advance in Ethical Analysis, which Aristotle had made, but on quite other principles from those in vogue among the following generation. Much was done more especially by the Stoics to deepen and strengthen moral speculation, yet these advantages were purchased by the sacrifice of a large portion of that wide field which Plato had vindicated for philosophy. This was inevitable. With a summum bonum constituted as theirs was, all that did not seem to serve to its attainment gradually ceased to be regarded; and that *all* was a great deal. Dialectic came to be absorbed in considering the rule which could regulate the conduct of a happy life: in other words, How is the individual to arrive at truth or that portion of truth by which he can guide his action? What is the criterion of truth? While the theory of cognition thus becomes the chief part of Metaphysics, indeed the only part very warmly and constantly discussed, everything else with the exception of the Aristotelian Logic, which the Stoics adopted, was supplied by borrowing, not as one might expect from

Plato and Aristotle, but from the speculations of an earlier date. Outside of the Lyceum and the Academy the thought of the day was almost pre-Platonic. The Epicureans revived the Atomic Theory of Democritus, the Porch fell back on the doctrines of Heracleitus: so great indeed was the influence of the latter, that in the hands of Ænesidemus, Scepticism but forms an introduction to the Heracleitean doctrines. The adaptations thus made were not always brought into complete harmony with the rest of the building. The Greek mind which, as Brandis observes[1], lost its "verve" and its individuality, the more it became involved in the task of spreading civilization in the Oriental and Roman world, seems to have shrunk from attempting to do anything further than roughly alter for its purpose the material it found ready to its hand. Its real interest was concentrated on the practical philosophy. And this in its turn drew its inspiration from other than Platonic or Aristotelian sources, from those in fact who, making the *individual* Socrates their model, had thereby given to their theories an individualistic tinge. The Stoics may be said to have been descended in the direct line from Antisthenes the disciple of Socrates: Epicurus, who railed against Aristotle, derived his ethics and his sensationalism from Aristippus. By the side of the dogmatic philosophies Scepticism slowly arose, as thoroughly penetrated as they were, by the tendencies of the

[1] *Handbuch*, III. 6, p. 1.

times, and like them more closely connected with the Imperfect Socratics than with any other of the teachers of the past. But, while the Stoic and the Epicurean always remained faithful to their early traditions, Scepticism was not and could not be the constant profession of any sect, it varied as its professors: and less rigidly formulated and strong from its very variations, it was destined to outlive its early opponents. It will be the endeavour of the following pages to trace its doctrines and its history—the scepticism of Pyrrho as distinct from the scepticism of Arcesilaus, and the relation of both to Scepticism revived under the Roman Empire. But as scepticism always is more impressed than dogmatism by the circumstances and feelings of the time, it will be most necessary to bear in mind the temper of the age in which Pyrrho lived, for then only can we understand why it took the course it did, and why ancient and modern scepticism, so similar in many particulars, yet differ so profoundly.

PYRRHO AND TIMON.

PYRRHO, the son of Pleistarchus, or, according to Pausanias[1], of Pistocrates, was born at Elis. Very few particulars of his life have come down to us, and those few we owe chiefly to the compilation of Diogenes Laërtius. Of humble origin, he is said to have been originally a painter, and a picture of some torch-bearers attributed to him was preserved in the gymnasium of his native place. He studied philosophy under the Democritean Anaxarchus; and it would seem that Democritus was his favourite among the thinkers who preceded him: the story of his having been a pupil of Bryson the son of Stilpon must, as Zeller[2] has pointed out, be rejected as chronologically impossible. With Anaxarchus he travelled as far as India in the train of Alexander the Great. On his return to Greece he settled in Elis, and lived there in honourable poverty with his sister Philistia, a midwife. His fellow-citizens gave him a priesthood, and on his account exempted all philosophers from taxation. He died at the age of ninety, somewhere probably between 275 B.C. and 270 B.C.

[1] Diog. Laërt. IX. 61; Paus. VI. 24, § 5.
[2] *Phil. der Gr.* II. a. p. 178. 3.

Pausanias saw his likeness in a porch by the agora, and a monument to his memory, which lay outside the city. His chief disciples were Hecataeus of Abdera, Timon of Phlius, and Nausiphanes of Teos, whom a doubtful report makes the teacher of Epicurus.

Such was the uneventful life of the man who has been generally regarded as the father of Scepticism. The name of Pyrrhonean will always adhere to the school: yet even in antiquity the position of Pyrrho was not undisputed, and that more particularly by the Sceptics themselves. They were anxious to claim for their views an earlier origin, and in consequence we find Theodosius of Tripolis expressly declaring that Pyrrho had no particular view of any kind, far less the right to give his name to the school, and Sextus Empiricus opens his "Hypotheses" with a long list of those who were Pyrrhoneans before Pyrrho. At first sight such objections may be regarded as valid; but I believe that, in this case at least, general tradition has not been in error.

Few words have suffered more from the licence of usage than Scepticism. It is indeed used so frequently as if it were coextensive with doubt, that it is now too late to hope it will ever be reclaimed and more accurately applied. Yet it is but a portion of doubt. In the history of philosophy doubt appears when Philosophy has separated itself from Theology, and so begun to be. Still that is not scepticism, and still less can the name be given to that wider form of doubt[1] that first breaks in upon and destroys the undisputed supremacy of belief—a supremacy that once contested can never regain its old absolutism. This general mistrust or doubt gains in definiteness, as it becomes more confined to a special object, and three branches may be singled out, as at any rate the most important: doubt applied to a body of facts or statements, doubt applied to the supernatural, and doubt applied to a subject that embraces all others— philosophy as the science of the Necessary. Taking the last as an example, we have, succeeding to the vague questionings, which are the first promptings to reflection, the more pronounced doubt which is provoked by a formed system of affirmative conclusions. Then isolated arguments crop up, which are mostly used by one who is merely clearing the ground to make room for a rival dogmatism; but which sometimes spring from a mind that looks with little confidence on dialectic. Lastly, the scattered objections are gathered up, and fashioned into a united array of argument: the doubtful neutrality or fitful raid gives place to regular warfare, and scepticism exists in the true sense of the word. The other divisions of doubt are both affirmative in their results. Rationalism tends to eliminate the supernatural, but at the same time to maintain the phenomena. The facts are still asserted, but with a new interpretation, and usually

[1] Hegel, *Werke*, XIV. 5. 42.

the value attached to them is different. Criticism
endeavours to sift the false from the true, and by the
very act of so doing it assumes that the true exists,
an assertion which scepticism would not deny, and
that moreover the true is accessible to us, an
assertion which scepticism would dispute. Criticism
can go further than scepticism. Antinomies ($\pi\alpha\nu\tau\grave{\iota}$
$\lambda\acute{o}\gamma\psi$ $\lambda\acute{o}\gamma o\nu$ $\emph{i}\sigma o\nu$ $\grave{\alpha}\nu\tau\iota\kappa\epsilon\hat{\iota}\sigma\theta\alpha\iota$, Sext. Emp. *P. H.* I. 12)
have long been a cherished weapon of the sceptic, but
they were, he believed, insoluble. When the critical
method was at last applied to philosophy, Kant carefully formed the Antinomies; but he also solved
them. For the sake of clearness these three kinds of
doubt may be enumerated, and rationalism and criticism, the two, which lead to positive results, distinguished from scepticism; but practice and advantage
alike forbid us to lay any great stress on the distinction. Scepticism, for instance, can hardly come
into being without some antecedent criticism, and
we often find the whole three prevailing simul-
taneously, and professed by the very same thinker.
Scepticism, as a formulated system strictly opposed
to dogmatism, really belongs to a comparatively late
period in the history of philosphy—a fact in itself
nearly enough to show how unfounded after all is
Bayle's remark, that scepticism is easy. Nor is most
of the abuse commonly lavished upon it much more
deserved, for it no more springs from the evil side
of man's nature than dogmatism does. Its great

vice is not its origin but its one-sidedness. It is inevitably one-sided, as it renounces part of the field of human knowledge: of its own free will abandons much that is valuable, and, distrusting some of the faculties, with which the mind is gifted, affords it only a partial cultivation. Hence, as Herbart[1] well says, "His thoughts are not come to maturity who persists in dogmatism." While however scepticism is harmful to one who never rises above it, it is of immense value to every beginning of inquiry, and its services in this respect have been recognized by all great thinkers, by none more than by Aristotle. The Nemesis of dogmatism, it is yet essential to the dogmatist, and of itself can hardly be said to have an indispensable existence. It is not a thing to be invented by any one man: it naturally rises up by the side of the systems it combats. From them it derives form and colour; changes as they change; grows as they grow; decays as they decay. It uses their arguments, borrows their methods, and adopts as it pleases their premises or their conclusions.

The foregoing remarks appear to be borne out in Greek history. Zeno of Elea and Heracleitus are among the earliest of those to whom the name of Sceptic has been applied with some show of plausibility, yet, when we come to sift such accounts, as have been handed down to us, we see that Heracleitus

[1] *Werks*, 1. p. 62.

denied all permanent Existence, only that he might affirm the principle of Becoming, and that Zeno, while he argued against Motion, asserted the doctrine of pure simple Being. The same remark applies to Xenophanes and Parmenides. Each was in reality a dogmatist, and sceptical only to the overthrow of what opposed his own speculations, and, though they greatly promoted scepticism, they promoted it unconsciously. But the generation which followed, a generation which delighted to call in question all that tradition and custom had combined to hallow, was not neglectful of the powerful aid, which the Eleatic and Heracleitean reasonings could lend to its general assault upon all objective truth. Zeno had shown Motion to be a dream: Heracleitus had shown Being to be a fiction. No wonder they were useful allies. The object of the Sophists was destruction, and they welcomed all that might help them to destroy, and passed by all that might help them to construct. How then, it may be asked, did the Sophists differ from the Pyrrhoneans? They were alike anxious to subvert, and alike hostile to the dogmatic systems of their times: nay from one point of view the Sophists are the stricter sceptics of the two. The Pyrrhoneans propose a practical end; they are sceptical not from love of truth, but from love of happiness: but the Sophists had no such end in sight. Whatever the failings and fallacies of particular teachers, the characteristic note of the school at large is a

c

restless thirst for progress and for knowledge, a daring wish to subdue all things to the individual reason. Nor is it enough to answer that the Sophists are after all not really philosophers, that they formed no system, that their theories and doctrines are obvious and trivial, for however much such accusations may tell against the majority of the Sophists, they can hardly be considered to affect Gorgias or Protagoras. The real ground of difference lies in the systems they severally attacked. In the Pre-Socratic period Dogmatism was based entirely on the objective, that is to say, objective realities were the sole recognized source of knowledge. When the Sophists confounded their opponents by the aid of the principle of subjectivity, they were doing, what Sceptics always have done, using one positive principle to overthrow another, but then (what true Sceptics do not do) they accepted as true the principle which had been their instrument. They used it sceptically, but enounced it dogmatically, and, although what they built up seemed at the time trifling in comparison with what they had pulled down, their positive doctrines became in the hands of Socrates a portion of a dogmatic system, and more especially inspired the philosophies which the New Academy assailed. Between the age of the Sophists and of Pyrrho, Dogmatism advanced greatly towards consistency and completeness, and almost by a natural law Scepticism shared the advance. It not only benefited by the differences that arose among the Dogmatists themselves and by the fruitless ingenuity of the Megareans, but it became consistent and complete, for it ceased to be sceptic on the one side, dogmatist on the other; it disputed the possibility of subjective, as much as of objective, truth; and so wide was its range, that, had it not been regarded only as a speculative means to a practical end, a philosophy that taught the great secret of how to be happy, Pyrrhonism would have been very closely akin to the doubt of modern times. One cause at any rate was conspicuous at its birth, which has been common to Scepticism in its rudest and most perfect forms, that feeling of despair which comes over the minds of those who have witnessed the failure of a great effort in philosophy; for then ensues deep distrust of the faculties, which have dared so much, and to all seeming achieved so little.

> "We rest our faculties
> And thus address the gods:
> 'True Science if there is,
> It stays in your abodes;
> Man's measure cannot mete the immeasurable All.'"

The depression was great, when the cosmologies had to be abandoned: it was still greater, when the speculations of Plato and Aristotle ceased to be satisfactory. It is clear from the tenor both of his life and of his doctrines, that Pyrrho despaired of philosophy, and was content to despair. M.

Saisset[1] has compared his early wanderings with those of Descartes; but the parallel cannot be extended further: Pyrrho returned from Asia with the conviction that truth was as yet not attained and perhaps unattainable: Descartes lived to vanquish the scepticism of Charron, and found modern philosophy. Talking of his life at Elis, Mr Lewes[2] has drawn a brilliant parallel between Socrates and Pyrrho and marked the superiority of the former in his life and in his death, but he has forgotten that, if Socrates is a far higher character than Pyrrho, the Greece of the time of Socrates was nobler than the Greece of the time of Pyrrho. Pyrrho did not oppose his age nor rise very greatly above it, and was so much admired, just because he so nearly fulfilled the ideal of his age. His rule of life did not however differ very widely from that of the Stoics or the Epicureans: it was, as has been already remarked, animated by the same motive as theirs, the same desire of escaping from the contact, if one may so phrase it, of the external world. It won, to be sure, the applause of Timon, and the absurd stories that Diogenes Laërtius relates, destitute as they probably are of foundation, still serve to show in what light it was regarded by Pyrrho's own generation or by the one immediately succeeding: and yet it may be safely asserted that, were there

[1] *Le Scepticisme*, p. 50.
[2] *Hist. of Philosophy*, I. 237.

nothing more novel or individual in Pyrrho and his teaching than an apathy which some have fancied was borrowed from the Indian Gymnosophists, he would not hold a more notable place in the history of philosophy than Ariston of Chios, with whom Cicero so often couples him. But we cannot accept the judgment of Pyrrho's contemporaries: Pyrrho's real merit lies not in the practical consequences to which his speculations led, but in the manner in which he commenced them, in the conception he formed of the task before him. According to Timon, Pyrrho declared that the philosopher should ask three questions[1].

1. How are Things constituted?
2. In what relation should we stand to them?
3. What will result to us from our relation to them?

The problem of philosophy is here proposed, as Erdmann has remarked, very nearly in the terms used by Kant; but the words prefixed, which describe the questioner as "he who would be happy," recall us from the great thinker of the 18th century to the contemporary of the Stoics. The answers show in a few words the essential points of Pyrrho's scepticism.

(1) Cognition, whether through the Senses, or the Reason, is not to be trusted, for the former gives us a knowledge not of Things as they are in them-

---

[1] Aristocles, *ap. Euseb. Pr. Ev.* 758 c.

selves, but only of phenomena, and the latter rests on conventional association, and not on scientific proof: nor is an attempt to combine sense-knowledge with Reason of any avail. Therefore our sensations and opinions are neither true nor false. Things in themselves lie beyond our sphere, equally indifferent (ἀδιάφορα), immeasurable (ἀστάθμητα), and undistinguishable (ἀνεπίκριτα).

(2) If the nature of Things be beyond our knowledge, we can form no opinion regarding them: we cannot distinguish the false from the true, for both to the senses and the reason all things are alike: they possess no criterion of truth[1]: we must not hazard those decided judgments, in which the dogmatist indulges: we must incline neither to the right hand nor to the left: we must remain unmoved (ἀδόξαστοι, ἀκλινεῖς, ἀκράδαντοι). We cannot assert of the individual object, that it exists or that it does not, for we are conscious only of our sensations: we allow that we see and apprehend the seeing, but we do not know the manner of sight or the manner of apprehension: it is phenomena only that we know. An object appears to us white, but we cannot be sure that the reality corresponds to the appearance. This is expressed in the famous maxim οὐδὲν μᾶλλον. We have no *more* reason for predicating one attribute rather

---

[1] Diog. Laërt. IX. 92. The wording of the clause is evidently post-Pyrrhonean, but something of the kind seems necessary to the argument, and is suggested by the "ἀνεπίκριτα" of Aristocles.

than another: we cannot affirm an object to be white: we can merely say that to us it appears white. In such circumstances only one position is possible to the philosopher: he is compelled to say "οὐδὲν ὁρίζω." In such a balance (ἰσοσθένεια) of evidence or rather in such a lack of all decisive evidence he must "refuse his assent" and suspend his judgment—an attitude, which under the names of ἐποχή, ἀκαταληψία, ἀφασία the Sceptics have extolled as the highest of human wisdom.

(3) The answer to the third question is a necessary consequence of the answer to the second. We have only to remember that the three problems were supposed to be put before one who was seeking for happiness. The third question then really amounts to this. What effect on our happiness will our attitude to Things have? This attitude has already been determined to be suspension of judgment. If therefore we are to make a rule of abstaining from all judgments, our happiness must be dependent on this abstinence, and consist in regarding everything external with undisturbed tranquillity of mind (ἀταραξία); for there is no certainty with regard to what is external, and, where there is no certainty, there can be no happiness. The soul must retire upon itself, looking upon all outside itself as indifferent, and striving to become neither the slave nor the mistress of circumstances, but separate from, and independent of, them. As Timon says, the wise man should be—

ῥῆστα μεθ' ἡσυχίης
αἰεὶ ἀφροντίστως καὶ ἀκινήτως κατὰ ταὐτά
μὴ προσέχων δειλοῖς ἡδυλόγου σοφίης.
(*Frag. Mullach*, vv. 147—149.)

The answer to the third question shows the aim of Pyrrho's doubt: like all his contemporaries he searched for a summum bonum: he was not a sceptic in the modern sense of the word: he doubted because doubt appeared to give him the most secure promise of happiness. On the other hand his scepticism is neither a mere attack on certain systems, an attempt to upset certain premises or certain conclusions, nor does it proclaim the uselessness of Ontology, and confine us to enquiries supposed to be likely to be more fruitful of results: such a theory as Pyrrho's is no one-sided, half-hearted scepticism: its conclusions are sweeping in the extreme: it declares that to us *all* is unknown and unknowable. In polemic it is particularly formidable as its principles are eminently aggressive, and its method (παντὶ λόγῳ λόγον ἴσον ἀντικεῖσθαι) has the somewhat uncommon excellence of being rigidly deduced from them. For one who believes that on every question there is unavoidably a balance of evidence, that no deciding reason is forthcoming, and that no predicate is more tenable than its contradictory, it is certainly competent to meet every argument by opposing to it its contradictory, as equally valid and reasonable. It is plain how formidable an adversary might prove, who assailed all positions with equal impartiality, and apparently exposed no vulnerable points himself. We shall have abundant proof of this when we come to speak of the New Academy. But, when we consider Pyrrhonism in its results, the verdict cannot be so favourable. On its principles, as Aristocles[1] has pointed out, science of every kind is an impossibility. Investigation cannot exist, when we are unable to show, why a thing is, rather than is not, why we affirm or deny it, or even to furnish a reason for the "why" itself. And this is true not in metaphysical questions merely, but also in those moral ones, which formed the staple of speculative enquiry among Pyrrho's contemporaries. For, when once the theory was laid down, that all that is external to us is indifferent to us, the numberless questions arising out of the practical applications of moral philosophy were swept away: there was no need of debating, how a man ought to act under such and such circumstances, when any possible course of action can have scarcely any possible effect. Such a position at once separated the Pyrrhonists from the rival Schools, and cut them from what was to the others the field of literary activity. No treatise similar to Crantor's on "Grief," and to that of Panætius on "Duty" could legitimately proceed from sceptics. But Pyrrho did not only run counter to all the tastes and tendencies of his time, he proposed an ideal that, while it wanted the attractions of Epicureanism, and failed to make

[1] *ap. Eus. Pr. Ev.* 762, d. cf. 759 c.

that appeal to many of man's noblest feelings, which won Zeno so many converts, was also in the highest degree unnatural. It did indeed meet the popular demand for freedom from the rule of the external, and although Pyrrho's own manner of life (διάθεσις) was much admired, the indifference he taught was so fettering, aimless, and deadening, as to meet with few imitators. Pyrrho himself felt the difficulty when he admitted "It is hard to strip off the man," and the later Sceptics toned down the original doctrine of ἀταραξία, and drawing a distinction between matters of opinion, and matters of necessity, (i. e., those on which they supposed themselves subject to outward influences) they sought for ἀταραξία in the former, in the latter they allowed that peace so perfect, inaction so complete could not be realized, and were satisfied to aim at μετριοπάθεια. As matters of necessity (τὰ κατηναγκασμένα), they reckoned the constitution of the individual man, and the manners and customs of society[1].

The modification just mentioned I would follow Zeller in considering as the work of the later Sceptics: however to justify the opinion it is needful to examine the question of the authorship of the various doctrines that we find gathered together in the treatises of Sextus Empiricus. In many cases Sextus does not refer to their authors the theories he states: in others his dictum is opposed to that of our other authorities.

[1] S. Emp. *P. H.* L 24, 25.

On this difficult and disputed subject I feel disposed to propose the two following canons.

(1) That all elaborated formulæ of sceptical argument and doctrine are to be ascribed to the later Sceptics.

(2) That the elements of Scepticism are nearly wholly Pyrrho's and not Timon's.

The first of these canons has in its favour that it asserts a process of development; common to most systems, and which is seen very distinctly exemplified in the New Academy and the Porch: indeed, when we remember how comparatively rude and superficial a doctrine Stoicism was, as promulgated by Zeno, and how small a length even Arcesilas carried the movement he set on foot, it is not apparently a very violent hypothesis, that Pyrrho only sketched the broad outlines of the philosophy which bears his name. Even the view, which I have endeavoured to disprove, and which was held by some of the ancients, that Pyrrho was not the founder of the Sceptical school, tends to show that he could not have been the author of a very complex body of speculations. "Beaucoup de bons esprits avaient douté avant Pyrrhon; mais personne, avant lui, n'avait élevé le doute au rang d'une méthode[1];" but then I believe he gave little more than the method. It is nearly certain that he *wrote* nothing except a poem addressed to Alexander, and a thinker, who thus neglected

[1] Saisset, *Le Scepticisme*, pp. 50, 51.

the ordinary means of spreading his opinion, and in this respect at any rate presents a strong contrast to the majority of the Post-Socratic teachers, who were, as a rule, somewhat voluminous authors[1], can hardly be supposed to have done more than trace the outlines for others to fill up. Instruction that is wholly oral can never be very intricate in its nature. Nor again is it likely that one who by all accounts lived a retired life and purposely settled at Elis, far away from intellectual controversies, could have engaged in the lengthy controversy with all known schools and sciences (particularly the polemic against Logic) which fills the eleven books of Sextus Empiricus *against the Mathematicians.* Indeed that he should have attacked the Stoics or Epicureans at all, is on chronological grounds extremely doubtful. Pyrrho was settled at Elis shortly after B.C. 323, and Zeno did not in all probability begin to teach much before B.C. 300, while Epicurus only opened his school at Athens in B.C. 306, and some years should be reckoned, as having elapsed, before Pyrrho could have gained familiarity with their doctrines. In fact we have no proof that he ever heard of them. Another argument for the canon is that, if we go carefully through Sextus Empiricus, and the abstract of the lost work of Ænesidemus which Photius has preserved for us in his Muriobiblion (*Cod.* 212), besides

---

[1] Yet Arcesilas and Carneades did not write. Cleitomachus published the doctrines of the latter.

being struck by the amount that has been borrowed from the New Academy, and from Carneades in particular, we are astonished to find how little there is that is even referred to Pyrrho. The polemic on Causality belongs to Ænesidemus, so do the famous ten Tropes[1]: the reduction to five was made by Agrippa, and they bear traces of a later phase of thought and doctrine than that of Pyrrho's day though even they were occasionally called Pyrrhonean.

It is more difficult to show plausible reasons for the second canon: it rests greatly on the light in which we regard Timon, the only one of Pyrrho's pupils who is of any importance to the historian of philosophy. Timon[2], the son of Timarchus, was born at Phlius somewhere between 325 and 315 according to Zeller. Originally a dancer, he was at one time a pupil of Stilpon, but admiration for Pyrrho drew him to Elis, where he lived some time with his wife, and where his children were born. Driven from this seclusion, by straitened circumstances it is alleged, he wandered about the Ægean Sea, the Hellespont and Propontis, and perhaps most of the Western Coast of Asia, and became known both to Antigonus and to Ptolemy Philadelphus, for the kings of the new monarchies had already become patrons of literature. Settling finally at Chalcedon he gained a high reputation as a Sophist, but, when he had earned a considerable fortune by his profession, he removed to Athens,

[1] S. Emp. adv. Math. VII. 345.   [2] Diog. Laërt. IX. 109.

and, with the exception of a brief sojourn at Thebes, he dwelled there till his death. His works were numerous, and it was doubtless through him that Pyrrho's doctrine became first generally known; but, apart from the consideration, that, if we assign the foundations, so to speak, of Pyrrhonism to Pyrrho and its further developments to the later Sceptics, there is little left to attribute to Timon, there is much reason to doubt the thoroughness of his discipleship. Pyrrhonism is in harmony with what we know of Pyrrho's life, greatly at variance with what we know of Timon's. General disbelief may have been congenial to a general railer; but what trace of "ἀταραξία" did he display? Proud, restless, bitter, physically deformed, and perhaps sensitive to his deformity, he tried every variety of poetry, and found himself most at home in parody and satire. In his most celebrated work, his Silli, he filled one book of narrative verse and two of imaginary dialogue with lampoons on all dogmatic philosophers (βεβλασφήμηκε παντὰς τοὺς φιλοσόφους). Personality was apparently his favourite weapon. Aristotle is accused of thoughtlessness (εἰκαιοσύνης ἀλεγεινῆς), Euclid of wrangling (ἐριδάντεω Εὐκλείδου), Zeno of intolerance (πάντων ἐπιλήπτορ); Pyrrho alone he reverenced partly for his tranquil life, partly for his skill in argument. "No one," he declares, "could contend with Pyrrho," but for any additions to Pyrrho's teaching we should hardly look to Timon. What Pyrrho did, can be told in a few words, and at first sight may seem but a small achievement: "he raised doubt to the rank of a method." It is probable that Pyrrho himself started from that portion of his theory which relates to practice, from the third and not from the first question: but however that may be, the more we consider his three questions the more we see their importance. They relate of course to the old points: "Is knowledge absolutely relative? Is there any objective truth? Can we have any knowledge of Things as they are in themselves?" but now for the first time do we find doubt possessed of a regular form. We have however Pyrrho's method alone before us: no notice of his application of it has come down to us: we do not know how he used it against the Ideas of Plato or Aristotle's conception of Matter: we first find it employed by Arcesilas against the Stoics. In Pyrrho's Scepticism and that of the New Academy is comprised almost all the Scepticism that Greece produced. I shall now proceed to trace the history of the latter. A knowledge of what it did and a slight discussion of what those taught, who under the Roman empire professed to revive Scepticism, will enable us to contrast Pyrrhonism and the Academy. More particularly shall we be able to compare the whole doctrine of the latter as exhibited by Carneades and Cleitomachus with the whole doctrine of the former in its last and fullest developement. Such a contrast ought also to throw light on the dogmas assailed as well as on the doubters who were the assailants.

THE NEW ACADEMY.

ARCESILAS the son of Seuthes or Scythes was born at Pitane in Æolia, about B.C. 315[1]. He learned mathematics from his countryman Autolycus, and, when Autolycus left Pitane for Sardis, Arcesilas was his companion. Afterwards his elder brother and guardian Moireas sent him to Athens to study rhetoric. He soon, however, turned to philosophy, and, when he had for some time been a pupil of Theophrastus, he passed over to Crantor and the Academy. On the death of Crates (in what year is not known), he succeeded to the headship of the school. It was a critical moment in its history. The Platonists were Platonists in very little but in name. Speusippus and Xenocrates had, it is true, greatly altered the doctrines of their master: but they had at any rate preserved the wide domain he had originally won for philosophy; and they were themselves men of much metaphysical ability. After their death the Academy yielded to the tendencies of the time; ontology was abandoned, and ethics formed the only portion of philosophy to which much attention was directed. The Academy ceased to have a definite doctrine, and its leaders, sometimes approaching the

[1] Diog. Laërt. IV. 28.

asceticism of Zeno, sometimes reverting to a more genial doctrine, made their teaching little more than a reflex of their personal characters. Consequently Arcesilas became head of a school, which possessed great traditions, yet had lost the power of competing successfully with the youthful vigour of the Stoics and Epicureans, and some change was imperative, if he did not wish to see the Academy fall into oblivion. He had the choice of a vigorous assault on the new system or facing again the old problems of subject and object, form and matter: but it was not a question for much hesitation: the spirit of the age was unfavourable to a new dogmatic philosophy; and the genius of the man pre-eminently adapted to polemic. Handsome in person, eloquent of speech, witty, and fertile in resources, he had all the gifts necessary for argument, and he would appear to have entered into it with zest. Naturally Stoicism had to bear the brunt of the attack. It was the most ambitious of the dogmatic systems, and therefore the most vulnerable, and such was the prowess and adroitness of the assailant, that his opponents compared him at one moment to the Empysæ, at another to the hydra of the legends. In manners and disposition he was the antithesis of the ascetic Zeno. Courteous, generous, and open-hearted, he was a thorough man of the world; fond of art and literature, he shared the love of luxury, common to his age, and was not too much of a philosopher to disdain altogether the complaisance of a courtier. Zeno has been likened to a Genevese Calvinist: we might compare Arcesilas to a Florentine in the palmy days of the Medici: but the scandal, which would distort these traits into faithlessness, drunkenness and servility, may be safely rejected, as the offspring of that rancour, which too often marked the rivalries of the Athenian schools,—a rancour which sometimes nearly equalled the fierce hatreds of Corenzio and the Neapolitan painters of the 17th century. Let us rather believe the testimony of Cleanthes[1] in favour of one, whom Timon satirized when living, but praised when dead. Nor do we need any story of youthful jealousy between Zeno and Arcesilas to enable us to account for their differences in later years. The conflict with Stoicism was unavoidable, for it grew out of the position, and, one may say, necessities of the Academy, yet it was a conflict that Plato might have shared in, for between Plato and an Empiric like Zeno there could have been no terms of peace. As chief of the sect, which beyond all others enjoyed the prestige of a glorious past, Arcesilas had the wisdom to conceal his innovation under the pretext of reviving the teaching of the founders of the school, and Cicero, in the character of Lucullus, compares him to the Tribunes, who pretended that their factious measures were such as would have met with the sanction of Publicola and Flaminius[2]. He carefully

---

[1] Diog. Laërt. VII. 171.   [2] *Acad. Quæst.* II. 5. 13.

collected sentences from Anaxagoras, Democritus, Parmenides, &c. as well as from Plato and Socrates, which countenanced his distrust of sense-knowledge. For Plato he professed a great reverence, and it is an old idea, supported by Geffers with much ingenuity, that he really wished to re-introduce the Platonic philosophy, and that his scepticism was but intended to smooth the way for the positive doctrines that he desired to establish. That an apparently thorough-going scepticism is, by some freak in logic, occasionally not incompatible with the acceptance of a dogmatic system is shown by the case of Ænesidemus: but, as regards Arcesilas, there is no proof strong enough to overcome the antecedent improbability. For what does the direct evidence consist of? A report mentioned by Sextus Empiricus and the same story told by Diocles of Cnidos. All that is supposed indirectly to favour the idea can quite as fairly be interpreted to mean that Arcesilas, in spite of the scepticism he introduced into the Academy, still retained the name of Platonist, and this is not only confirmed by the testimony of Numenius the historian of the Academy, but by the evidence of the Pyrrhonists themselves. Timon, his contemporary, did not forgive the inconsistency as he deemed it of one who seemed to be preaching Pyrrho's doctrine from the chair of Plato, and, whom Ariston, the Stoic, parodying the verse of Homer, declared to be—

"πρόσθε Πλάτων, ὄπιθεν Πύρρων, μέσσοι Διόδωροι."

The supposition of Tenneman[1] that Arcesilas had never heard of Pyrrho cannot be accepted, but the question of the measure of his indebtedness will be best discussed, when we come to consider the difference between the Academy and the Sceptics.

With Arcesilas commences the New or, as some have called it, the Second Academy, which began that contest with the Stoics, which Numenius compares to the battles of the Trojans and the Greeks. Under the pretext of reviving the Socratic method of questioning, Arcesilas suppressed the lectures, which were the customary mode of teaching at the Academy, and substituted for them a discussion between himself and his hearers on the several topics he introduced. Thus the whole training that he gave appears to have been intended to fit his pupils for controversy, and, as the Stoics before the time of Chrysippus were deficient in readiness and in command of words, he rapidly gained a superiority which Zeno vainly attempted to counterbalance by writing against Plato and affecting to ignore Arcesilas.

Scepticism, says Sextus Empiricus, is "ἀντιθετικὴ φαινομένων τε καὶ νοουμένων καθ' οἷον δήποτε τρόπον," and this is the point in which Arcesilas attacked Zeno. The question in dispute is in fact the great question of the time, "What is the criterion of Truth? what is the connection between Phenomena and Noumena?" The mind, said the Stoics, is

[1] *Gesch. d. Philosophie*, IV. p. 190.

at birth like a blank sheet of paper that receives representations (φαντασίαι) made by the direct agency of the object (φανταστόν), and all our knowledge is therefore in its origin derived from the senses. From perception springs memory, and from the memory of several similar perceptions — experience (ἐμπειρία). Conclusions, drawn from experience form concepts, which are another source of knowledge: drawn naturally and without the aid of method, they are the general ideas (κοιναὶ ἔννοιαι—προλήψεις), which the Stoics regard as the natural laws of truth and virtue —drawn methodically and consciously they constitute science, which alone gives irresistible conviction. The representations furnished by the senses are received as *knowledge* (in contradiction to opinions), only after they have been submitted to the understanding. True impressions are those, which, when thus submitted, are found not merely to be impressions, but to awaken in us an irresistible conviction that they present to us the real. Such a representation is called an intellectual representation (φαντασία καταληπτική); and this intellectual representation is the criterion of truth.

But a criterion of this nature Arcesilas'[1] will not accept. At the first glance he cannot admit, as the arbiter of truth and falsehood, a conviction, which belongs as much to the fool as to the wise man. For in the wise man it is knowledge, in the fool opinion, and

[1] S. Emp. *adv. Math.* VII. 153—158. Cf. Cic. *Acad.* II. 24. 77.

yet the difference is only nominal! Besides, if we accept the Stoic classification the words involve a contradiction. Apprehension (κατάληψις) is an act of assent, and assent, according to the Stoics, is an act of the understanding, not of the perception. To their notion, that the strength of the conviction was a guarantee, so to speak, of reality, he replies with the favourite Pyrrhonic argument, maintaining in various ways, that there was no true representation such that a false one could not be equally well formed. Having thus, as he supposed, refuted the argument for sense-knowledge, Arcesilas considered himself to have shown the impossibility of all knowledge, apparently not regarding at all the possibility of knowledge through the reason. The Stoics had laid great stress on the distinction they drew, and which was universally accepted, between knowledge and opinion: the former alone is worthy of the wise man. If then, so Arcesilas put the question, knowledge is impossible, what is left to the wise man? Can he trust himself to mere opinion? must he not take refuge in a total suspension of judgment (ἐποχή)? If his opponents attempted to escape from this conclusion by an appeal to practical life and its necessities, Arcesilas would not allow that the will could not be exerted and that action became an impossibility, if certainty were taken away from us. There is no real dilemma: between action under the guidance of full and perfect knowledge, which to man is unattainable, and all cessation from action, which to man is impossible, lies a third, the only practicable course. A representation calls the will into play, apart from any consideration of its truth or untruth: *Probability* is a *sufficient* guide for the conduct of life. "The man, who[1] suspends his judgment on all matters, will," says Arcesilas, "rule his choices and his refusals, and his actions generally by the probable, and, following that as a criterion, he will fare well. For happiness is won by prudence, and the province of prudence is right action. Now that is rightly done for the doing of which a probable cause can be rendered. He then, who gives heed to the probable, will fare well and be happy." Thus far we are able to follow Arcesilas: but here on the borders, so to say, of ethical philosophy, our information fails. The few scattered hints, which have been collected from Plutarch and Stobæus by the skilful industry of Zeller, are insufficient to inform us of the manner in which he criticized the Stoic Ethics, Physics, Theology and Logic, and make us feel how great an evil is the fragmentary state, in which Cicero's Academics have come down to us. I am disposed to believe that, what pass for the arguments of Arcesilas, represents rather the general teaching of the Academy previous to Carneades, that is to say, under Evander and Hegesinus, for it appears to be directed against a more developed form

---

[1] οὐ...ἐντύχων κατανοεῖ the reading of the MSS. seems contrary to the sense intended, yet so Fabricius, Bekker, and Geffers.

of Stoicism than that of Zeno and Cleanthes. However the data are too few to allow of anything beyond the merest conjecture: we know very little of Lacydes: Evander and Hegesinus are to us mere names, and we are compelled from lack of knowledge to pass on at once to Carneades.

Carneades, the son of Epicomus or Philocomus, was a native of Cyrene, born like Plato, as his admirers were fond of remarking, on the day[1] of the Carneia, a festival of much importance in a Dorian city. While still young, he seems to have gone to Athens, where he became the pupil, and in course of time the successor of Hegesinus. But his chief instructors were the Stoics he combated. He studied Dialectic under Diogenes of Babylon, and he pored over the works of Chrysippus, to whom indeed he felt so deeply indebted, that he was fond of applying to himself the common saying,

"εἰ μὴ γὰρ ἦν Χρύσιππος, οὐκ ἂν ἦν στοά,"

by changing the last word:

"εἰ μὴ γὰρ ἦν Χρύσιππος, οὐκ ἂν ἦν ἐγώ."

When he became head of the Academy, he soon restored its reputation which had decayed after the death of Arcesilas, and such was the charm he exercised that some of his rivals quitted their own schools to go and listen to his lectures. He took part (B.C. 165) with his former teacher Diogenes, and Critolaüs the

[1] Plut. *Qu. Conv.* VIII. 1. 2. (717. a).

Peripatetic in the well-known embassy, which the Athenians sent to Rome to deprecate the heavy fine imposed upon them for their treatment of their old possession Oropus. It is hardly necessary to repeat the tale, how Carneades on the one day gained the approval even of Cato the Censor by his eloquent declamation in praise of Justice, and how on the next he shocked him by refuting his former argument. It is a story that reads more like a page out of the life of Gorgias in the 5th century than of Carneades in the 2nd. Latterly subject to many infirmities which he is said to have borne with impatience, he expired in the 85th year of his age, B.C. 129. In opinions he was the true representative of Arcesilas, in subtlety and width of view he surpassed him as he probably surpassed all philosophers who came between Aristotle and Philo. At the same time it should be borne in mind that he only trod in the path first shown by Arcesilas, and that if his philosophy is much in advance of his predecessor's, the advance was, as he himself allowed, greatly owing to the immense improvements that the Stoic philosophy had received at the hands of Chrysippus. Chrysippus had refined the materialism of Zeno, deepening and ennobling both his ethics and Metaphysics, and the arguments of the Academy required a corresponding reform to be enabled to meet Stoicism in its new guise. But Carneades was not satisfied with a mere critique of one dogmatic system:

Scepticism with him has a wider range and a higher aim, and in this point he rose as much above Arcesilas, as he probably fell below him in that winning address and grace of manner and speech, which we know of only by tradition, and which are utterly lost in the meagre outline of his theories, which is all that has survived. Carneades, absorbed in his own thoughts, shunned society, disregarded his personal appearance, and seemed unconscious of what was passing in the world about him. Yet such was his energy and eloquence, aided by a very powerful voice, that he was the most impressive orator of his age. Like Arcesilas and Pyrrho he wrote nothing, but in Cleitomachus he had a disciple fully able and willing not to let his name perish.

In detailing the philosophy of Carneades it will be convenient to divide it into two parts (A) Destructive (against the Dogmatists), (B) Constructive.

(A) The Destructive relates principally to :
    (1) The theory of Cognition.
    (2) Ethics.
    (3) Theology and Teleology.

(B) The Constructive relates to :
    (1) The theory of Probability.
    (2) Ethics.
    (3) Theology.

Carneades, as we shall see hereafter, was averse to physical enquiries. Logic seems to have been more particularly the province of Cleitomachus.

(A) (1) Arcesilas had confined himself to a polemic against the Stoics: the critique of Carneades is directed against dogmatism generally, and his followers so far imitated him as to examine each system in detail, and were indeed accused of a tedious minuteness (S. Emp. *adv. Math.* IX. 1), though Stoicism was to them as to their master the principal aim of their attacks. If we contrast the following critique on the possibility of cognition with the objections urged by the earlier philosopher, we at once see this enlargement of aim combined with greater thoroughness of investigation, yet it is substantially the result of a similar train of thought[1]. Carneades[2] begins with a general statement that there can be no criterion of truth, whether we suppose it to be reason, or the senses, or a representation, for they all alike deceive us. The intellectual Representation of the Stoics *represents* falsehood as well as truth. But even, if Representation can furnish a criterion, this criterion cannot exist apart from the affection of the mind caused by the presence of the object. It is the possession of senses that distinguishes what is animate from what is inanimate, and it is through the senses, that man apprehends both himself and the external world. But the senses are not senses, and are incapable of apprehension, if they remain unmoved and impassive: it is by their being moved and acted on by the

[1] Cic. *Acad. Quæst.* I. 12. 46.
[2] *Ib.* II. 13. 40 and 14. 47, &c. S. Emp. *adv. Math.* VII. 159.

presence of the object, that they indicate the object. The criterion must therefore be sought in the affection of the mind by the presence of the object, and this affection must indicate both itself and the object whose appearance causes it. Now this affection is nothing else than the representation. But like a lying messenger the representation often presents the object otherwise than it is in reality, and is at variance with what has sent it. We cannot therefore accept every representation as a criterion of truth, but that representation only which is true.

Having thus demonstrated that not a representation quâ representation, but only a *true* representation can be accepted as a criterion, Carneades proceeded to state the four following propositions.

(1) There *are* false representations.

(2) Such false representations may pass for true.

(3) If two representations present no distinguishing marks, they cannot be regarded, the one as true, the other as false.

(4) There is no representation by the side of which cannot be placed a false representation, which is notwithstanding indistinguishable from the true.

The first proposition has been assumed in the foregoing argument; and was disputed by no philosopher, except Epicurus: the third was allowed on all hands: the second and fourth were the contested points, and it was on them that Carneades and his disciples loved to expend their ingenuity: they defined and analysed with a confidence in their own theories which to their opponent Antiochus seemed in strange contrast to the scepticism they professed: but the last, the old objection of Pyrrho and Arcesilas, seems to have been regarded as the most cogent and important; and, when Cicero is speaking in defence of the Academy, it is the only one that he allows is questioned. It was much insisted upon by Carneades, and supported by him with those arguments from the *abnormal*, which are always in favour, when Psychology is in an imperfect state. In dreams and visions, we are moved by false representations, as powerfully, as if they were true: madmen too are the prey of such delusions: Hercules destroyed his own children under the firm belief, that they were the children of Eurystheus. Nor are the general Ideas and Concepts of the Understanding, which, as derived from Experience, the Stoics valued as so authoritative, more trustworthy than the Sensual Perceptions. Objects may be so similar in shape and appearance, that they cannot be distinguished from one another. Even a poulterer can often not tell one egg from another. Lysippus may reproduce his statue of Alexander a hundred times yet no faculty nor representation enable us to decide which is a replica, and which the original. Nor are our judgments of form and distance, derived though they are from experience, by any means free from error. The perspective of a picture often leads the eye astray, the blade of an oar dipped in the water seems crooked: the sun's rays invest the dove's neck with a thousand unreal hues. Such are the results given by the Understanding when directed to objects of sense. Nor is it to be received as unerring in objects of reason. Alike in mathematics, in music, in letters, it is no infallible judge. In philosophy how many great problems are there which are still agitated and unsolved! How many different schools exist and have existed which not only disagree in opinion, but directly contradict one another. Even in minor questions, it has failed to bring certitude. That favourite but dangerous instrument of Chrysippus the Sorites has shown, how hard it is to define and draw exact limits. In quantitative distinctions even he was forced to allow suspension of judgment under the title of ἡσυχάζειν, and to decline to unravel his own puzzle whether three are few or many. It is therefore clear that philosophy is at best only a formal science: it arranges our thoughts, but it does not afford any information not derived from the senses, and in what is derived from them it affords no clue to distinguishing the false from the true. Neither then from the side of the Understanding, nor from that of the Perceptions, is knowledge possible, not even to the *wise* man of the Stoics.

(Λ) (2) Carneades, as has been already said, disregarded physics. We see in him therefore another proof of the gradual abandonment of that encyclopædiac position, so strikingly exemplified in Aristotle, and of the ever increasing preponderance of Moral Philosophy. The Stoics too made Physics in a large measure subordinate: they upheld the same ideas of law and order in the worlds of nature and of morals. Their theories therefore, so far as they may be said to have an ethical reference are sharply criticized by Carneades, and in truth this is the part, in which he is most sceptical: in *pure* Ethics, if one may use the expression, he was far more constructive than destructive. On such topics the little of his teaching, which is sceptical in its character, belongs to his celebrated speech at Rome—a speech which he may very probably have himself viewed in no more serious light than that of a rhetorical exercise. In it he employs the old sophistic cavils about Justice, contrasting justice and convention much in the fashion of the Callicles of Plato. It should be borne in mind that Carneades was addressing a Roman audience, one which held nearly the same views of right and wrong, as the Athenians did before the times of Gorgias and Protagoras, and that he would naturally use before it arguments, which in Greece would have been reckoned somewhat worn out and antiquated.

(A) (3) At any rate we find the criticism of Carneades at once more original and searching, when applied to contemporary theories—the Stoic Teleology and Theology. Of the stoic doctrines we have from various sources accounts of tolerable fulness and they are so familiar that it would be wasting space and time to detail them here: for the objections urged by the New Academy Cicero[1] is our chief and (except in the discussion of the Divine Attributes) nearly our sole authority. Sextus Empiricus, who treats of the matter in a somewhat cursory manner, ascribes them to the New Academy generally, but Zeller[2], who has gathered together the passages of Cicero with great skill, no doubt rightly regards them as in the main the work of Carneades. They may be arranged as the stoic theories are in the following order:—

(1) The World—its providential government and its rationality.
(2) God—The proof of His Existence.
The Concept God in itself.
The Polytheistic theory.

(1) The idea of a providential government is as vigorously combated by the Academy as by the Epicureans. Had God made the world for man's good, would he have placed in it wild beasts, noxious vermin, poisonous plants, all alike harmful to man? Reason is called the noblest gift of God to man. When we see how men misuse their reason, we feel rather disposed to believe in improvidence than in providence, to wonder why God has given us at all, what is abused so much. "Sentit," remarks Cicero,

[1] *N. D.* III. 11.
[2] *Ph. d. Gr.* III. a. p. 460. 3, &c.

rising from the prose of the dialogue to the rhetoric customary to his speeches, "domus unius cujusque, sentit forum, sentit curia, campus, socii, provinciæ, ut, quemadmodum ratione recte fiat, sic ratione peccetur; alterumque et a paucis et raro, alterum et saepe et a plurimis." All the crimes and tragedies of our race have been the work of beings possessed of reason, and would not have been possible without the aid of reason. You may throw the blame on the vices and errors of men, but why not give them a reason that would exclude vices and errors? The Stoics declare Folly to be the greatest evil, yet even they allow that there is no wise man to be found. If, then, Folly is a greater evil than all calamities of fortune and body, in what a wretched plight we must be, and if the Gods have denied to *all* men the blessings of wisdom and virtue, why have they denied happiness to the virtuous man? Here we find the Academy asking the old question, which has tried the faith of so many. Why should virtue and happiness be so little connected? The lot of the just man is often misery: the bad man enjoys the fruits of his wickedness. And this, too, not in small matters only—the drought that withers the crops or the hail that breaks the vine—but in the lives of great men, in the exile of Africanus, in the deaths of Scaevola and Socrates. Dionysius had a prosperous reign of eight and thirty years, though a tyrant and a plunderer of temples: the murderer of Scaevola died in his bed, consul for the seventh time! Even if the criminal meets with punishment, his crimes are often such as no punishment can compensate for. Prevention would surely have been better.

Granting that the stoic view is correct, that there is design evidenced in the economy of the world, that, as Chrysippus maintained, the pig exists to be slaughtered and eaten, that the world is the most beautiful and best world possible, all this may be explained without the hypothesis so much dwelt on by the Stoics, of a God who is the world's soul. Cannot the framework of the world be explained, as the work of Nature, acting in accordance with natural laws? It is impossible to prove that the Divine interference is necessary to the regulation and existence of the Universe: many, on the contrary, have, like Straton of Lampsacus, held that the Gods abstain from all interference with it. If regularity is a mark of divine origin, we must ascribe tertian and quartan fevers to divine interference. The truth is that so little do we know of the matter that either opinion can be entertained. These mysteries, for they really are mysteries, continues Carneades, and lie beyond the limits of our knowledge, are such that we cannot penetrate them: we do not understand our own bodies; far less the earth or the moon or sun, which we cannot dissect or anatomize. No wonder then that there are such monstrous and contradictory theories. The syllogism of Zeno is simply worthless. He argues thus:—

> The rational is better than the irrational.
> Nothing is better than the world.
> ∴ The world is rational.

Following such a model of reasoning one can prove the world to be an excellent reader—

> The literate is better than the illiterate.
> Nothing is better than the world.
> ∴ The world is literate.

Nor is the reasoning of Chrysippus much better. "If," he urges, "there is something, which men cannot bring about, he, who brings it about, is superior to man. Man cannot bring about the things which are in the world. Therefore he, who has been able to bring them about, is superior to man. Now who except God could be superior to man? It is therefore God." But in both syllogisms the objector remarks the words "better," "superior," "Nature" and "Reason" are used without any attempt at accurate definition: it is assumed too that the only being higher than man is of necessity God: why should it not be nature? Nor is there much more force in another proposition put forward by Chrysippus. "If a house were beautiful, we should perceive that it was built by its masters not by mice. So therefore we should consider the world the *home* of the Gods." This would be valid if Chrysippus could demonstrate that the world was *built*, not *formed* by nature. As for the question of Socrates, "whence have we derived our soul if there be none in the world?" one might as well ask, whence we derived our speech, harmony or song.

(2) The stoic theory of the *World Soul* might lead us to suppose that the stoic Theology was pantheistic in character. In much the same spirit God is also identified with Fire, Æther, or an all pervading vapour. The expressions of Cleanthes in his wellknown hymn are, on the whole, quite compatible with pantheism, and it seems to me very difficult to suppose that Carneades considered the Stoics not to hold the ultimate identity of God and the world: yet when Carneades examines the Stoic conception of God, his arguments are mainly directed against a personal Deity. We must carefully remember that he has discussed the peculiarly Stoic views in talking of the World-Soul: in the critique of the concept of a First Cause, he has in view the more common notion of Deity as well as the Stoic one. As has been already said, he discusses, firstly, the proof of His Existence, then the concept God in itself, and then the polytheistic theory. Carneades has already discussed the theory of God as connected with the world: he now passes to the proof of His Existence *per se*, which the Stoics rested upon the argument drawn "e consensu gentium," that is, from the universality of the belief. They supported this by arguments, from the internal, from the feelings of piety, and holiness and of reverence for God which men feel and which presuppose God's existence, and from the ex-

ternal, from omens, auguries, &c. But, urges Carneades, the Stoics are wrong as to the fact; we know that there have been Atheists, and of the opinion of many nations we know nothing: so we cannot assert the universality: and yet, if we could, we cannot accept the judgement of an unreasoning multitude. As for the omens and auguries, their truth is doubtful; there may be a few instances of successful prediction, but they are at best happy accidents: divination has no proper province: it has no application to the knowledge obtained through the senses, or to science or philosophy, or state affairs: in necessary results it is of no avail: in accidental it is impossible.

In treating of the concept God, he concerns himself with the attributes commonly ascribed to God, particularly immortal, all-good, and all-knowing, and the somewhat rude anthropomorphism, which he evidently takes for granted even at the outset, is justified, when compared with the grosser terms that were often employed. Every living Being must have a Sensual Nature: nay, if all-knowing, must have even more than the ordinary five senses (for both parties hold all knowledge, if attainable, to be attained through the senses) and be capable of sensation, and consequently of change in the soul, all sensation producing, according to Chrysippus, a change in the soul. What is capable of sensation, is capable of perceiving the harmful, as well as its opposite, and change, produced by the harmful, is a step towards destruction. Liability to change therefore precludes the idea of immortality. Nor on the other hand can we conceive of a material nature that is indivisible, and so secure from decay. Therefore immortal cannot be predicated of God, and certainly mortal cannot. It is just the same with the other two contradictory attributes infinite and finite. Infinity is incompatible with the idea of motion, for motion must always be in space, that is, within limits also. Finite cannot be an attribute of God, for the finite as the part is inferior to the Infinite as the whole, and by the stoic hypothesis only what is best and most excellent can be ascribed to God. If then in the case of both pairs neither of the contradictory attributes can be predicated of the subject, there can be no subject for predication. Hence, considering God as a living Being, the only possible conclusion is Atheism. If we consider him as a rational Being, we must attribute to Him happiness and virtue, for the former cannot exist apart from the latter. But God, as all-virtuous (πανάρετος), possesses all virtue. Now virtue implies an imperfection overcome. Continence supposes possible incontinence, endurance possible weakness: Courage possible cowardice. We obviously cannot ascribe such attributes to God: they are the qualities of those who are liable to temptation, and temptations, involving, as they do, change and decay, belong only to mortals: Mortals alone can suffer from passion or danger. We are equally at fault if we predicate practical wisdom (φρόνησις) or prudence (εὐβουλία) of the Deity. Practical wisdom involves the knowledge of things good and evil and of such as are styled indifferent (ἀδιάφορα), and thereby of pleasure and pain, for pain springs even from things indifferent. But a knowledge of pleasure and pain is as impossible to one who has not experienced the pleasurable and the painful, as a knowledge of colours to a blind man. But God has never experienced the painful and can therefore have no idea of pain, and as pleasure is merely the removal of the painful, pleasure is also unknown to Him. Prudence involves deliberation and deliberation the existence of something obscure. A Being therefore who deliberates must find that much is obscure, and cannot be supposed to have certainty on the most obscure point of all, whether or not, at some time or other, something will lead to his destruction. But a being, to whom this rests a problem without solution, must ever be a prey to fear and therefore mortal.

We may pass over some other objections where the difficulties stated are only verbal, and pass on to one of greater interest and validity. "Can we ascribe speech to God?" To deny it to him is absurd, yet the other alternative is only apparently more simple. Speech involves vocal organs, and such a conception would lead into absurdities worthy of Epicurus, anthropomorphism of the worst: Speech must be the speech of some nation—Greek or foreign, a supposition equally monstrous in such a case. And finally having shewn that it is impossible to limit the Infinite by attributes, and, that, the moment we endeavour to do so, we run ourselves into contradictions of the most hopeless character, Carneades briefly dismisses the most limiting attribute of all—corporeal as of all the most incompatible with the idea of immortality.

He naturally proceeds from this question to the consideration of the ordinary Polytheism, which the Stoics defended, partly because it testified to that universal belief in a Divine Being, which they regarded as the strongest evidence of His existence, partly because it tended to preserve that respect for Order and Law, which they always inculcated in their Ethics. Carneades' answers were couched in the form of soritæ—one of which at least, we are informed, Cleitomachus greatly admired. It runs somewhat thus and turns upon the ordinary personification of natural elements as Divine Beings. If Jupiter is God, his brother Neptune is God, if Neptune, Achelous, if Achelous, the Nile, if the Nile, any river, if any river, any mountain stream ($ρύαξ$). But mountain streams are not Gods: neither is Jupiter God. Again if the Sun is God, the Day (i. e. the sun above the horizon) is God; if the Day, the Month, if the Month, the Year a collection of Months. But the Year is not God: neither is the Sun God. Divination, as we have seen, found no more favour with Carneades than any other portion of the popular belief: he rejected alike the popular theology and the Monotheism of the philosophers. His polemic against the latter I have given in a very bare outline, but the principle involved in it is easily understood: he denies the existence of God, because we cannot think of the Infinite without giving Him attributes, and the giving of these attributes at once involves us in absurdities. It is curious to observe how far Carneades has anticipated much of mediæval and modern metaphysic: his theories when translated into English run almost insensibly into the most modern of philosophical language. The argument from design had been already so clearly stated by Aristotle, that we do not wonder at finding it criticized. In regard to the concept of God the first step had of course been made, when Xenophanes rejected with horror the popular conceptions: Aristotle had done still more, when he dwelt on the difficulty of ascribing virtues to Him, and carefully eliminated as many attributes as possible from the Conception of the First Cause. Carneades was however the first to seize on the difficulties which surround the problem, difficulties that had indeed been made more evident by the Stoic Theology. Many of his proofs are little better than fallacies of a tolerably transparent kind, but such imperfections are due partly to the time, when words often took the place of things, and partly to the difficulties of a first attempt. He did not understand the contrast between the human and the divine: with him the divine differs from the human in degree not in kind. So far his conception falls below not only the Platonic but also the Aristotelian. The Deity he rejects is after all only a man, with more than a man's might and much of a man's caprice, and, while he saw the absurdity of the *details* of anthropomorphism, he never rises above a conception, which is at bottom anthropomorphous. Indeed, though I have translated ἄπειρος by infinite, indefinite would much more accurately express the meaning of Carneades: τὸ ἄπειρον is not used by him in the Pythagorean or Aristotelian sense, nor is it the modern infinite: the finite with him is merely a part of the infinite, that is, indefinite; a whole which may or may not be limited, but which is not by any means incapable of limits. If Carneades had had an adequate conception of the First Cause, he would never have supposed that he had answered the Stoics, when he substituted nature for God. He does not appear to have appreciated at its true value the higher side of their doctrine, a divine spirit of Law and Order working in the world: he never attained in fact to the idea of Cleanthes,

"Ζεῦ, φύσεως ἀρχηγέ, νόμου μέτα πάντα κυβερνῶν."

But Carneades finds his justification in the lower side of Stoicism. His dim perception of a natural growth apart from any Divine providence is lofty, when compared with a gross confusion of God and matter which degraded the divine without raising the material: if he is mistaken in rejecting their appeal to the universality of the belief in a God, many illustrious names have shared his mistake, and it was the more pardonable in his age as the Stoics themselves had done their best to discredit à priori philosophy. The speculation of Carneades only needed a more propitious time to have achieved far greater results: as it is, if inferior in some respects to the noblest form of the Stoic doctrine, it was far more correct logically and possessed far more capability of developement.

(B) (1) The positive side of Carneades' theories, so far as they have a positive side, is almost wholly practical and ignores all higher speculation. He accepted and enlarged the doctrine of Probability, as the true rule of life, which Arcesilas had put forward, when he rejected as impossible a criterion of knowledge that would at the same time suffice as the guide for human conduct. Like Arcesilas too, he had denied not merely that any representation could give us certainty, but that all representations were of equal value. The Academy and the Porch agreed in believing that knowledge comes through representations, and therefore it became incumbent upon one, who started from the premises of Arcesilas, and did not regard these representations as of the same worth, to arrange them according to the importance, which ought to be accorded to each, that is to say, to classify and discover the amount of probability belonging to them severally.

And this was to the Academy a more weighty matter than we might at first be disposed to believe, for one is apt to forget that by their denial of certain knowledge, they had left themselves nothing but probability. A representation according to Carneades has a twofold relation, one to the object it represents, another to the person to whom it is a representation. In the former relation, it is true, if it coincides with the object, untrue if it does not, in the latter it may appear true or appear untrue. That which appears true, possesses probability ($\pi\iota\theta\alpha\nu\acute{o}\tau\eta\varsigma$, $\emph{ἔμφασις}$) and is a probable representation ($\pi\iota\theta\alpha\nu\grave{\eta}$ $\phi\alpha\nu\tau\alpha\sigma\acute{\iota}\alpha$); that which appears untrue to us, whether coinciding with the object or not, possesses improbabilities ($\mathit{ἀπειθής}$, $\mathit{ἀπέμφασις}$), and is an improbable representation ($\mathit{ἀπίθανος\ \phi\alpha\nu\tau\alpha\sigma\acute{\iota}\alpha}$), exerts no influence on our actions and cannot be a criterion of truth. Of the former class some for various reasons, the smallness or remoteness of the object or defect of vision in the observer, are indistinct, and on that score they too may be omitted, not being capable of serving as the criterion, for neither the object represented nor the representation are sufficiently brought before us to influence our actions; but the criterion of truth is found in others, which, both appearing true, and being distinct, may according to their probability be separated into three grand divisions, each of them admitting of subdivisions. To begin with the lowest form of the criterion—when a representation itself excites a belief in its own truth without, however, possessing any extraneous support, it is termed "probable;" when it stands in connection with and is confirmed by other representations, it is termed "probable and unimpeached" (ἀπερίσπαστος); when these concurrent representations individually bear examination, it is styled probable, unimpeached, and tested (περιωδευμένη). Thus the highest amount of probability is the result of cumulative evidence: this is inevitable, for the separate representations may be false without our being able to detect the falsehood. To one or other of these three divisions we ought to refer the circumstances amidst which we live, for an unconditional "yes" or "no" is more than our faculties warrant: all that we are able to do is to attach a tolerably accurate value to the "perhaps," and the more important the question, the more accuracy ought we to endeavour to obtain. In matters of but slight moment the first grade of probability will suffice, for those of greater consequence the second; the third Carneades would reserve for those which were in his eyes and in the eyes of his contemporaries the most weighty, those which pertain to happiness.

(B) (2) As might readily be conjectured, the Ethics of the Academy are much coloured by this theory of probability: but we are ignorant of the manner in which it was applied: the senses can, except on the Epicurean principles, be no source of knowledge in ethical matters, and, as Zeller remarks, it is very difficult to understand on what grounds Carneades rested his scheme of Probability and distinguished the various grades of it. We could not consistently look for a subjective criterion. Yet not only did he extend his doctrine of Probability to moral questions, but he expressly defended the freedom of the Will against the Stoics, and according to the account given by Cicero in the fragment that has come down to us of his treatise "De Fato" (§ 31 cf. § 23), he rested his argument on the *fact* that there are things which are in our own power. If all things are the results of antecedent causes, all things are but links of a chain of causes and effects, and necessity is all powerful: but this is not so, for some things are in our own power, and our will is not the result of antecedent and external causes. It seems almost impossible to reconcile either of these positions with the rest of what we know of Carneades' philosophy, and certainly the conjecture of Zeller, that he regarded the freedom of the will as only probable, seems opposed to what little information we have on the matter.

As regards the conduct of life, we do not find that Carneades dogmatically selected and proposed a Highest Good as the aim of life. The art of living—for Carneades, differing in this respect from the Pyrrhoneans, does recognise an art of living—cannot, any more than any other art, dispense with a moving principle, and therefore an ideal is requisite to give to action first an impulse and afterwards consistency. The problem is approached with some caution, and Carneades begins by laying down two requisites essential, in his opinion, to the concept of the Highest Good. (1) It must be accordant with, not opposed to nature: (2) it must be capable of exciting a craving in the mind (ὁρμὴ, adpetitus animi). He finds only three ends, or rather motives, which fulfil these conditions. They are Pleasure — Freedom from Pain — Things the most simple and natural (prima secundum naturam), such as Health, Beauty, &c. We may regard either the attainment of one of these ends or a life regulated by conformity to one of them as the Highest Good, so that, as each of the ends can be viewed in this double aspect, there are in all six possible Ideals. It is evident that our choice of an Ideal will greatly modify our whole theory of Right and Wrong: for instance, if pleasure be our aim, our conception of right will inevitably be based upon our desire for pleasure. Further than this, Carneades did not go: he pointed out the results of a selection but he declined to commit himself to one, though he warmly defended that of Calliphon,— "pleasure combined with virtue[1]," and Cleitomachus professed himself ignorant of his master's real opinion. Such an attitude, which however the Sceptics censured

[1] It is a vexed question what place virtue held in the Ethics of Carneades: Cicero's accounts are somewhat contradictory. Zeller (III. a. p. 475) conjectures him to have held that Virtue consisted in activity directed to the attainment of what is agreeable to Nature, and that it was not separable from this the Highest Good.

as too affirmative for a sceptic, was the almost unavoidable consequence of the situation of the Academy. Carneades could not fix on any particular Good without openly becoming a dogmatist: he could not deny the existence of a Highest Good without placing himself in direct and violent hostility to his own age. Now and again he seems to have espoused some one or other of the many fancies, which were put forward on this the favourite problem of later Greek philosophy, but he more generally contented himself with rebuking the extravagances of the contending sects. More especially when viewed on this side, his teaching is marked by much of that sanity, which had formed so glorious a feature of Greek thought in all its inquiries during its earlier and better days, but which had been greatly weakened by the decay and disintegration, that had been the fate of Hellas under the Macedonian rule. He deprecated the endeavour to live very strictly and narrowly in accordance with a preconceived system, and found fault with the way, in which the Stoics appeared to glory in trampling upon the real needs and weaknesses of man's nature, and throughout, his views, if not so noble in aspiration, had more real humanity than theirs[1]. Cicero reports that it was owing to his keen polemic, that they modified the rigour of their doctrine, and allowed to external reputation ($εὐδοξία$), which they had hitherto affected altogether to despise, an independent

[1] Compare the story in Cic. *Tusc.* III. 59.

value of its own, by placing it among things *desirable*[1]. The wise man, he maintained, sometimes indulges in *opinion*[2] (opiniatur): he is affected but not crushed by circumstances; and with that lack of or rather contempt for patriotism which was common to his age, he told the Carthaginian Cleitomachus that he thought a philosopher would not be greatly troubled if his native country were conquered. Great warmth of feeling was inconsistent with a system, which was founded on good sense: its more natural outcome was a sober moderation which neither rises to the sublime nor sinks into the extravagant.

(B) (3) Towards the popular theology Carneades preserved such an attitude, as might be anticipated. He had dogmatically rejected Monotheism, and after his reasonings in that discussion he should, to be consistent, have rejected Polytheism. He indeed ridiculed its personifications of the material elements, when they were defended by the Stoics, but from respect to popular prejudices, he refrained from open hostility to the popular religion, and claimed the sceptic's privilege of abstaining from giving a decided opinion for or against it. He neither, like Plato, cared for the truths disguised, but not wholly concealed, in its Mythology, nor, like Zeno, valued it for its old associations and present influence. He as far as possible disregarded it.

As might be anticipated, the New Academy paid

[1] Cic. *de Fin.* III. 17. 57.   [2] Ib. *Acad. Quaest.* II. 35. 112.

much attention to the Sorites and dilemma and the fallacies, such as the well-known ψευδόμενος, which arose out of them: but in spite of his dexterity in the use of Logic, Carneades apparently neglected its theory, and this seems to have been the peculiar province of his pupil Cleitomachus. A Carthaginian, and originally called Hasdrubal, he lectured on philosophy in his native city and in the Punic language. When forty years of age, it may be on the breaking out of the third Punic war, he repaired to Athens, where he attached himself to Carneades. A favourite pupil, he transmitted to posterity the doctrines of his master; and so indefatigable was his industry, that he composed no less than 400 books, one of which he dedicated to L. Censorinus, Cons. B.C. 149, and another to the satirist C. Lucilius. He died some time after B.C. 111, in which year Crassus the orator heard him lecture. He adhered closely to the doctrines that had now become identified with the Academy, though he was well versed in the Stoic and Peripatetic systems, and apparently wrote a history of philosophy (περὶ αἱρέσεων); and his Logic was accordingly formal in its tendency. Logic, he declared, is, as the Stoics assert, a part, and the Peripatetics assert, an instrument (ὄργανον) of philosophy, an instrument so far as its laws are formal and divorced from all consideration of things—so far as they are founded upon things, a part of philosophy. For instance, if you say, from two universal principles the conclusion is universal,

Logic is an instrument, but if you connect your syllogism with things, and state your universal premises and conclusions with regard to them—
 The soul is endowed with perpetual motion;
That which is endowed with perpetual motion is self-moved.
 ∴ The soul is self moved;
in such a case Logic ought to be considered part of philosophy[1].

Beyond this view of the functions of Logic we have little information about the logical efforts of Cleitomachus. He made Logic subservient to the Academic Scepticism, and we find him preserving the Sorites, with which Carneades attacked Polytheism, and he probably followed him in his onslaught on the ἡσυχάζειν, that quaint device by which Chrysippus thought to ward off his favourite form of syllogism when directed against himself.

With Cleitomachus Scepticism ceased in the Academy; those who came after him were Eclectics, men, who in the decay of philosophical thought endeavoured to form new systems by combining the labours of the past, not always with much heed as to the congruity of the elements they strove to mix together. Scepticism had failed to excite a reaction, and died out apparently from the want of a new dogmatic system to attack: we shall pass on to its revival under the Roman Empire.

---

[1] See the quotations in Prantl, I. p. 499, n. 5.

THE LATER SCEPTICS.

HOWEVER important to the general history of Scepticism, the later Sceptics can find place in this Essay only so far as they were *Pyrrhoneans*, that is, filled up the outlines of Pyrrho's doctrines and persevered with the work he had commenced. Between him and them too elapsed a considerable portion of time, though the exact date of Ænesidemus the first reviver of Ancient Scepticism has been much disputed: their last important representative Sextus Empiricus can be placed with tolerable certainty in the first half of the 3rd century. Fabricius[1] conjectures that Ænesidemus flourished a little before the time of Cicero: his evidence is a passage quoted from Ænesidemus by Photius in his Muriobiblion: "οἱ δ' ἀπὸ τῆς Ἀκαδημίας, μάλιστα τῆς νῦν, καὶ Στωικαῖς συμφέρονται ἐνίοτε δόξαις, καὶ εἰ χρὴ τἀληθὲς εἰπεῖν, Στωικοὶ φαίνονται μαχόμενοι Στωικοῖς." This he supposes to be a reference to Antiochus, one of Cicero's instructors, who, as is well known, though head of the Academy, approximated in his speculations somewhat closely to the Stoics. L. Tubero, to whom Ænesidemus dedicates his Πυῤῥωνίων λόγοι, is said to be Cicero's

[1] *Ad S. Emp. P. II.* i. 231.

friend Lucius Ælius Tubero. This conjecture has however been rejected, and I believe justly, by Ritter and M. Saisset. If a distinguished philosopher, as Ænesidemus by all accounts was, had been engaged in reviving Scepticism in Alexandria in Cicero's youth, we can hardly believe that Cicero would class Pyrrho and Herillus together as "diu abjecti," or call his philosophy "jamdiu fracta et extincta," and the doubt is, I think, confirmed by the absence of any mention of Ænesidemus in Seneca. M. Saisset would therefore refer his date to the end of the first century of the Christian Era; but even this, I think, is too early. Aristocles says: "ἐχθὲς καὶ πρῴην ἐν Ἀλεξανδρείᾳ τῇ κατ' Αἴγυπτον, Αἰνησίδημός τις ἀναζωπυρεῖν ἤρξατο τὸν ὗθλον τοῦτον." Now Aristocles (according to the correct reading of the text[1]) was the master of the Aphrodisian, who flourished in the reigns of Septimius Severus and Caracalla, and cannot be placed much before A. D. 170, which would certainly not allow us to put Ænesidemus before A. D. 130. The argument, that might be brought against this supposition derived from the list given by Diogenes Laërtius, is untrustworthy, as the list is certainly incomplete.

Pyrrhonism died out almost immediately after the death of Timon: it was not revived till Ænesidemus saw in it a fitting means of clearing the way for his Heracleitean theories: with those theories we have at

[1] Zeller, III. a. p. 701, n. 3.

present little concern: it is with his scepticism only that we have to do. His famous work the Πυρρωνίων λόγοι treated of metaphysical, physical, and moral problems: but the points of most importance are the ten tropes (τρόποι) and his argument on Causality.

The ten tropes[1] were intended to contain a refutation of Dogmatism in all possible forms.

The *first* has reference to the uncertainty of the senses, and the different ways in which different animals are affected by the representations of the same object. Some animals have one sense highly developed, some another.

The second continues this argument, the examples however being entirely drawn from men. Demophon the steward of Alexander felt, it is said, warm in the shade and shivered in the sun. Andron the Argive hardly felt thirst, and other such instances are quoted.

The third contains the same arguments showing that the same object appears in different aspects according to the sense to which it is submitted. An apple is yellow to the sight, sweet to the taste, fragrant to the smell: had we more senses we might discover other qualities.

The fourth enlarges on the dispositions of the subject, and the effect of such influences as sleep, waking, joy, grief, hunger, thirst, &c. When our states are so variable, we cannot know when we are in the proper state to judge rightly of things external.

[1] Diog. Laërt. IX. XI. 79; S. Emp. *P. H. I.* 40, 162.

Whatever criterion we offer requires proof, but an indisputable proof is impossible, for we have no criterion. We can therefore form no judgment on representations of what is without.

The fifth trope (in Diogenes Laërtius the seventh) begins the question of the relation of subject and object. Distance and position, roughly speaking, make an immense difference in the appearance of an object. Here we come on the objections of Carneades. The dove's neck varies as it changes: square objects sometimes appear round, straight ones bent, &c. &c.

The sixth trope refers to manner of perception: it reminds us that we see objects always through some medium, air, vapour, fog. Our eyes too, the instruments, are liable to water and to be covered by films; and the other senses, the ear and the nose, &c. are subject to various changes, all of which prevent our knowing the object as it is.

The seventh (in Diogenes the eighth) treats of the quantity and modes of the object. Things vary according to their quantity. Scrapings of goat's horn are white, the horn itself black: scrapings of silver black, a mass of silver white, and so with others. A small amount of wine strengthens us, a large amount weakens us.

The eighth (in Diogenes the tenth), in part a repetition of the preceding ones, dwells on the relativity of all phenomena. All objects are relative, firstly to the subject—secondly to one another. What is genus in one relation is species in another. The same man may be son, brother, father.

The ninth is on the strength of association. What is familiar to us excites no wonder in us: we admire what is strange because it is strange.

The tenth (in Diogenes the fifth) continues the same train of thought. It shows the influence of custom and law, religion and opinion, and the different standards of right and wrong adopted by different nations.

These ten tropes scarcely merit the reputation they acquired in antiquity: they do not contain anything that had not been at least as well said before, and they do not atone for their lack of novelty by any precision of scientific arrangement. In many of the latter ones we find partially repeated the substance of the former: it is difficult to detect either any order in their arrangement, or any regular process by which they have been reached. They all enounce more or less directly the relativity of human knowledge, but that is the only thread of connection which runs through them. Sextus would class the first four as relating to the judging subject, the seventh and tenth to the object judged, and the rest as relating both to the subject and object; but in one and all we miss any clearly drawn distinction of subject and object, any attempt to discriminate the nature of the antithesis between them, and the means of overcoming it.

THE LATER SCEPTICS. 73

The number of illustrations, with which Sextus Empiricus loads them, does not avail to disguise the fact that there is very little in them that had not been far more ably urged by the earlier sophists. The argument in regard to causality is, however, of more importance, and it is difficult to believe that it is due to the same author.

The following arrangement is due to M. Saisset[1]. Each proposition except the last contains at least two contradictory statements, both of which are refuted.

Proposition 1, comprising 4 hypotheses:

Hypotheses 1 and 2.—The corporeal is the cause of the corporeal.
The incorporeal is the cause of the incorporeal.

Disproof. If A were cause of B, it would produce it, either by remaining itself, or joining itself to C. In the former case it would produce nothing different from itself, for, suppose a unity A could cause a duality A, B, each element of this duality could cause a new duality, and so on *ad infin.*; in the latter case union of C with either of these two letters would produce a fourth, these a fifth, and so on *ad infin.*

The incorporeal, too, is intangible; it cannot act on another, or be acted on by another.

[1] *Le Scepticisme*, p. 153.

Hypotheses 3 and 4. The corporeal is cause of the incorporeal.

The incorporeal is cause of the corporeal.

Disproof. The incorporeal is not contained in the corporeal, nor *vice versâ:* or rather if the one be contained in the other, it is not produced by it.

Proposition 2. If cause and effect are both in motion, or both at rest, neither of these two terms can be the cause of the other: If one is in motion, the other at rest, neither can be cause of the other. For a cause only produces what is contained in its own nature, and here the two terms are heterogeneous.

Proposition 3. The cause cannot be contemporaneous with the effect, for then the effect would possess existence independent of the cause; nor anterior, for a cause without an effect is no cause; nor posterior, for in that case there would be an effect without a cause.

Proposition 4. The cause produces its effect itself, or produces its effect by aid of passive matter: the first hypothesis is contrary to experience: on the second the passive matter would be as much an agent as the cause proper.

Proposition 5. The cause has several powers, or it has one only. If only one, it would always produce the same effect, which is contrary to experience; if several, it ought to manifest all of them in its action, which is also contrary to experience.

Proposition 6. (1) The agent is separate from the patient.
(2) The agent is not separate from the patient.

If the first, the action of the one is possible without the action of the other. If the second, they will operate by contact; but the difficulties of such action are insoluble.

Proposition 7 forms a syllogism:

The cause is relative to the effect.

But relative ideas have only an imaginary existence.

∴ the cause has only an imaginary existence.

Sextus Empiricus fills a large part of Book 9, according to the ordinary numbering of his work, *Adversus Mathematicos* (§§ 142—330), with a dissertation upon cause and effect. After arguing at considerable length against causality, he adds that Ænesidemus had treated of the subject with more clearness, and proceeds to state the propositions given above (§§ 218—266). There are some lacunæ, Sextus adopting his usual plan of not repeating those points in an argument which he has happened to have stated already; but the purport and tendency of the two passages are very similar. It is unnecessary to repeat both; and M. Saisset has supplemented the lacunæ in the argument given to Ænesidemus, from what comes before it. They were probably taken from the fifth book of his treatise, which we know was entirely devoted to the subject. Throughout Ænesidemus presupposes the truth of Materialism. Hence he assumes, in arguing against the very first hypothesis he enunciates, the maxims: "A cause cannot produce that which is not contained in its own nature;" and "A cause must be tangible, i.e. act by contact." He shows this particularly in his second proposition, where he says a cause must either be in motion or at rest; evidently excluding thereby the possibility of the existence of cause and effect out of space. These materialistic hypotheses he uses in his first five propositions; assuming in each of them that contact is necessary to the action of a cause,—and in the sixth he turns round and denies it. He advances the exception commonly taken in antiquity to the possibility of contact; confusing the abstract notion of contact with the physical fact[1]. The seventh proposition is far more striking than the preceding ones. It shows that in the first six Ænesidemus was more or less directly combating what he saw to be an error, the giving an absolute value to the principle of causality; the selfsame error that Kant attacks in his transcendental dialectic. As a materialist he would necessarily suppose that, if he could show that causality has only a subjective value, he

[1] S. Emp. *ad Math.* IX. 252, &c.

had shown its absurdity. The very conclusion that he regards as fatal to the doctrine of causality is the one which Kant endeavoured to prove is the only tenable one; that causality is a condition, and a necessary condition, of thought. It is interesting to observe the difference between the scepticism of Ænesidemus and that of Hume. The former starts from a really materialistic point of view, and shows the absurdity of the doctrine of causality when upheld on materialistic grounds: the latter, starting from the standpoint of Locke (one in reality intellectual), destroyed materialism when he pointed out that we have no perception of the connection of cause and effect in the external world. Had Ænesidemus ever seen this it would have solved most of the difficulties at once; as it is, his speculations may be said to signalize the highwater-mark of Greek speculation in respect to causality: they have a universal interest that is wanting to a great deal of his own and of Carneades' polemic against the Stoics, and they involve far more real difficulties, far more clearly stated, than are to be found in his ten tropes. His so-called eight tropes deserve notice for the judicious and stringent character of their criticism, but belong rather to the history of the natural sciences than of Metaphysics. They are directed against that false method of preferring theory to observation, and of observing facts through the light of a preconceived hypothesis, which vitiated so much of the natural science of the ancients, and produced those strange contradictions which led Carneades to declare that science treated of what was beyond the reach of the human faculties. They stand solitary among the achievements of the Pyrrhoneans in this respect, that they are not sceptical but critical, not subversive but intended to reform a mistaken methodology.

We cannot accord to Ænesidemus the praise of consistency. As has been already mentioned, he used scepticism only as preparatory to a revival of the Heracleitean philosophy, and the opinions of Ænesidemus the Heracleitean are often curiously at variance with those of Ænesidemus the Sceptic. To the Heracleitean belong the doctrine that Time is τὸ πρῶτον σῶμα, the theory of motion and the assertion that the Understanding looks on the outer world through the medium of the senses. The Sceptic argues against the possibility of a criterion in the spirit of Pyrrho. Like him, he will not allow of knowledge through both the reason and the senses; they are in his view antagonistic, and the trustworthiness of the one necessitates the untrustworthiness of the other. Among the conflicting judgments of mankind it is impossible to find a sure criterion. The things perceived by the senses are either generic or individual; the latter can lay claim only to relative, not absolute truth, for the knowledge of man is relative. To prove the reality of a genus, one is compelled to mount up to the highest genus, what the Stoics call τὸ γενικώτατον.

Now the truth or falsehood of this would involve the truth or falsehood of all contained under it. Besides, how can the senses comprehend a genus? These arguments probably filled part of the fourth book of the great work of Ænesidemus, his Πυῤῥωνείων λόγοι, of which Photius[1] has given the contents. The first book was introductory, and stated the absolute scepticism of the Pyrrhoneans in the most unqualified manner; the second took up the True, Cause, Affection, Motion, Generation and Decay. To this book I am inclined to refer the eight tropes, though Fabricius would place them in book five; the third book treated of Motion, the Senses and their qualities; the fourth of the theory of Signs, Nature, the World and the Gods; the fifth of the theory of Causality already given; the last three books were ethical; the sixth treating of Good and Evil; the seventh of the Stoic theory of Virtues, and the eighth of the *summum bonum*. The arguments were apparently similar to those used by Sextus in the eleventh book of his treatise *Adversus Mathematicos*, and touched upon in the tenth trope. His conclusion is that only an end agreed upon by all men (such is Zeller's interpretation of the passage in Photius) can be accepted, and there is no such end. Ænesidemus also wrote *Pyrrhonean Outlines* and some works devoted to expounding his Heracleitean system.

This positive element which Ænesidemus at-

[1] *Bibl.* CCXII.

tempted to introduce into Scepticism was not accepted by his successors, and probably on this ground they were distinguished from him, and were alone in strictness called the later Sceptics, in contrast to the earlier Sceptics, among whom even Ænesidemus was classed. They too made some advances.

The famous ten tropes possessed no such internal coherence as to defy any attempt to abridge their number: we hear of a reduction of the ten to two: a more celebrated one is that of Agrippa, the fifth philosopher, we are told, in descent from Ænesidemus. In this reduction the original ten tropes are contained in the first and third tropes: the other three contain what, if not novel, was yet not included in the ten.

   I. (τρόπος ἀπὸ διαφωνίας). Dwells on the uncertainty of customs and opinions.

   II. (τρόπος εἰς ἄπειρον ἐκβάλλων). On the accumulation of proof: one proof requires another, and so on *ad infin.*

   III. (τρόπος ἀπὸ τοῦ πρός τι). Things change as their relations change.

   IV. (τρόπος ὑποθετικός). Truth is but hypothetical.

   V. (τρόπος διάλληλος). You prove the truth of the criterion, and then require a criterion to prove the proof.

The list of Diogenes Laërtius does not include Agrippa, though the tropes are ascribed to him in the life of Pyrrho. After Ænesidemus it contains no notable name till we come to the last but one, Sextus Empiricus. Like many of the later sceptics, a physician, and in spite of his surname belonging to the school of the Methodici, he wrote a considerable number of treatises, in which he gathered together the objections of all preceding sceptics. What remains to us is a work entitled the *Pyrrhonean Hypotheses*, in three books, and two others which are commonly joined together under the designation *Adversus Mathematicos*, and form eleven books. The *Pyrrhonean Hypotheses* are at once the oldest and best of these writings. They give an outline of the sceptical system, and the details are supplied in *Adv. Math.* Books VII.—XI. which form a direct continuation.

The first book of the *Hypotheses* is introductory, and opens with the definition of Scepticism, its nature and purpose (§ 1—35). The ten tropes are then given, and a curious psychological discussion interposed on the question, whether the lower animals are possessed of reasoning powers equal to man's or not : this question is decided in the affirmative (§ 35—164). The ten tropes are followed by Agrippa's five (§ 164—178), and the two (§ 178—180), and the eight of Ænesidemus (§ 180—187). The sceptical maxims are next discussed (§ 187—210), *i.e.* οὐδὲν μᾶλλον, κ.τ.λ.

The differences are pointed out between Scepticism and the systems that had been brought most nearly in contact with it. These are the follow-

G

ing: (1) the Heracleitean (§ 210—213); (2) the Democritean (§ 213—215); (3) Cyrenaic (§ 215); (4) Protagorean (§ 216—220); Academic (§ 220—236); and the Scepticism of the Empirical Physicians (§ 236 *ad fin.*).

Book II. commences the controversial portion of the treatise with a discussion of a question which might not unnaturally occur, whether the sceptic through his profession of ignorance is debarred from comprehending, and therefore discussing, the theories of the Dogmatists (§ 1—13). This difficulty disposed of, the subject is divided, as had been done by the Stoics, into metaphysics, physics, and ethics (§ 13). Of course the first thing mooted in metaphysics is the question of the criterion (§ 14—80).

The criterion is discussed, (1) in respect to the judging subject (τὸ ὑφ' οὗ); (2) the instrument of judging (τὸ δι' οὗ); (3) the object judged (τὸ καθ' ὅ). The reasons given for rejecting the criterion are, (1) In regard to the judging subject (or man) himself, as was shown in the fourth trope, philosophers are not agreed: his nature and powers are very variously defined, and we cannot be said to comprehend him. The very assertion, that man is the judge, is an assumption, and it is not agreed whether the judge is to be the individual man or a typical man (like the stoic wise man), or the majority of men (§ 22—48). Mankind will never unite in fixing on an individual whose opinion is to be accepted as decisive: the supremely wise man, supposing such a person to exist, will be too wise for the rest of men: from his very wisdom he will be able to make the worse appear the better reason: we cannot trust him: for the opinion of the majority Sextus has no more respect than Arcesilas. (2) The instrument of judging is shown to be untrustworthy, whether the senses or the intellect, or both (§ 48—70). The senses are criticised in the usual way: as to the intellect we know nothing of its nature: Gorgias believed there was no such thing: to Heracleitus it was all in all: the senses and the intellect are often at variance, and those of one person differ from those of another. (3) The object judged is discussed, but entirely with reference to the stoic theory of representation, and with arguments modelled after those of Carneades. After the criterion has been rejected, Sextus curiously thinks it necessary (§ 70—80) to discuss the possibility of truth (§ 80—97). Truth lies neither in the phenomenon nor in the ἄδηλον.

The mention of the (ἄδηλον) leads to a discussion of the stoic theory of signs (σημεῖα), and its rejection on similar grounds to those advanced against the criterion (§ 97—134). A sign, that merely acts on the law of association, which reminds us of what we have perceived in connection with it, Sextus allows of (σημεῖον ὑπομνηστικόν): a sign for the indication of what is obscure (ἄδηλον) he disputes (§ 104—134). It is (1) relative to the thing signified: (2) if objective it must be the same to all, if subjective (λεκτόν) it would itself need a sign. If there can be no sign, there can be no probation; and this leads Sextus to his well-known polemic against Logic, which is classified under the following heads:

> Probation (§ 134—193).
> Syllogisms (§ 193—204).
> Induction (§ 204).
> Definition (§ 205—213).
> Division (§ 213—219).
> Genus and Species (§ 219—229), and Accident.
> Fallacies (§ 229—259).

Probation cannot of itself give conviction; it has no virtue of its own; it is impossible to detect a fallacious argument, one in which there is no consecution between the premises and the conclusion, for we should require first to test the concatenation of the premises: there are no *à priori* forms of probation. A probation too is relative: the premises and conclusion are in a fluctuating relation and the relative *is* not; every probation involves an opinion, and an opinion is a matter of controversy. The validity of the syllogism falls with that of probation. Take

> All men are human beings
> Socrates is a man
> ∴ Socrates is a human being.

The major premise can only be posited after the fullest induction, which would involve the examina-

THE LATER SCEPTICS.   85

tion of the minor premise and conclusion. The syllogism therefore is a mere reasoning in a circle: this holds good too in hypothetical syllogisms. A complete Induction is impossible. Definition, Division, &c. are discussed mostly in reference to the Stoic Logic; Fallacies are rejected as being unavailable for the discrimination of truth and falsehood.

The third book opens with the question of causality, including the conception of the Deity as the First Cause (§ 1—30). The difficulties started have already been stated in speaking of Ænesidemus and Carneades. The next subject is comparatively poorly handled (§ 30—119). Material principles, such as those of the Ionic philosophers, are first stated and dismissed. Then matter and its modes are treated of in a perfunctory manner. Matter cannot be considered as agent and patient, for then a cause would be implied: considered in respect of its qualities, it is liable to the difficulties about contact used by Ænesidemus in reference to the theory of causality: besides, it cannot be classified among things sensible or things intelligible. After a number of quibbles about addition and diminution, &c., founded on the confusion of physics and metaphysics, Space and Time (§ 119—168) form, with Number, the conclusion of the section on Physics. The objections to Space, Time and Number, considered as objective realities, are urged with much skill and at some length; as to the first, however, Sextus allows that, while his argument tends the other way, space is too *present* to admit of the Sceptic's being sceptical in this instance.

Ethics (§ 168—279) he defines as concerned with the Good, the Bad, and the Indifferent. Seeing the number of opinions held regarding the Good and the Bad, he concludes, after a short dissection of the stoic theory, that the concepts Good and Bad rest on an artificial and not a natural basis. Where a Highest Good is proposed, the question arises, whether the thing striven for or the strife to obtain it, is the real Good. The latter is inadmissible, as there is an end beyond the strife, and the former, because men have entirely different conceptions of good. It is impossible to suppose that, what is *outside* the soul altogether can be the end that it strives for, and we know too little of the soul to hazard an assertion as to what is good for it. Its very existence is hypothetical. The idea, too, of this strife after good and of avoidance of evil upsets the whole peace of life, for it involves us in a chronic state of disquietude and desire for that which is never obtained. And the differences of opinion as to what is good and what evil are the cause of great diversities of national usage. Death seemed to Cleobis and Biton a great good—to some life is a great evil (§ 179—239).

"Ἰχρῆν γὰρ ἡμᾶς σύλλογον ποιουμένους
τὸν φύντα θρηνεῖν, εἰς ὅσ' ἔρχεται κακά.
τὸν δ' αὖ θανόντα, καὶ κακῶν πεπαυμένον
χαίροντας, εὐφημοῦντας ἐκπέμπειν δόμων."

The sceptic, seeing such confusion of belief and custom, will practise ἐποχή, and follow the ordinary manner of life. An art of living is impossible; for the duties of life fall upon the ignorant as well as the learned: more especially an art in the Stoic sense, for that involves an acceptance of the Stoic metaphysics. The refinements attempted by the Stoics have only led them into extravagances (§ 239—252). There can indeed be no teacher and no learner of an art of living (§ 253—273).

The outlines thus furnished in the *Hypotheses* are filled up in the treatise which forms the latter part of the work *Adversus Mathematicos*. The metaphysical topics fill books 7 and 8 of the ordinary numeration, the physical books 9 and 10, the ethical book 11. Valuable as a quarry for materials, these books have much less scientific merit than the *Hypotheses*. Though always a clear writer, Sextus has amassed a large amount of material, and put it together not always in good order, and often without much heed as to whether his work was internally consistent. Beyond good sense and clearness and industry, Sextus had not many of the qualifications needful to an historian of philosophy. The only dogmatic system he was thoroughly versed in was that of the Stoics. As M. Saisset has remarked, he evidently was very imperfectly acquainted with Plato; Aristotle he probably knew only at second hand, and even Epicurus he did not know well. The first two books contain a critique more curious than valuable on Grammar and Rhetoric; in the third and fourth Geometry and Arithmetic are criticised, most of the arguments being the same as Sextus employs in his books on Physics; Astronomy and Music occupy the fifth and sixth books, but the whole six really form a separate treatise, and have no proper connection with the last five. They are of small importance, and do not directly bear on the subject of this Essay. Besides them Sextus appears to have been the author of two other books, one called ὑπομνήματα, and another on the Soul.

In spite of the wide diffusion of the Pyrrhonean doctrines, especially among physicians of the Empirical school, in the second and early part of the third centuries, a fact to which Galen bears testimony, there is no distinguished name that we can add to the list of sceptics except that of Favorinus of Arelate the friend of Herodes Atticus and the teacher of Aulus Gellius, who introduced into the law courts the arguments of the New Academy. Between it and Pyrrhonism he appears to have wavered; we know he wrote ten books of *Pyrrhonean Tropes;* but all his numerous writings have perished, and there is no material for following the history of the School either in the period that elapsed between Agrippa and Sextus Empiricus, or in subsequent times. The canon, if we may so call it, of sceptical writers closes with Sextus. With the beginnings of New

Platonism we have as little concern as with the Eclecticism which intervened between Cleitomachus and Ænesidemus. Our material is complete, and it only remains to compare the New Academy with Pyrrho.

THE PYRRHONEANS AND NEW ACADEMY CONTRASTED.

IN the introduction to his account of the Pyrrhonean doctrines Sextus is, as we have seen, careful to distinguish them from those of other philosophers, separating them from the Heracleitean philosophy which had been connected with it by Ænesidemus, from the Democritean, which Pyrrho himself had studied and admired, from the Cyrenaic, to the ethics of which they somewhat approximated, from that of Protagoras, who took so considerable a part in the first revolt against Dogmatism, and lastly from the Academic. This is the question I now propose to enter into. It is one that was much discussed in antiquity as well as in modern times. To pass over Timon's attacks on Arcesilas whom he declared to be in reality a Pyrrhonean, Ænesidemus at the outset of his work observes:

"οἱ μὲν ἀπὸ τῆς Ἀκαδημίας δογματικοί τέ εἰσι καὶ τὰ μὲν τίθενται ἀδιστάτως τὰ δὲ αἱροῦσιν ἀναμφιβόλως· οἱ δὲ ἀπὸ Πύρρωνος ἀπορητικοί τέ εἰσι καὶ πάντων ἀπολελυμένοι δογμάτων."

And in conformity with this we find Sextus Empiricus

asserting that there are three classes of philosophers: the Dogmatists who declare that knowledge is attainable, the Academics who deny that it can be attained, and the Sceptics (ζητητικοί, quæsitores) who are engaged in the search for it.

Aulus Gellius devotes a short chapter of the *Noctes* to the discussion of the point. "Vetus," he begins, "quæstio et a multis scriptoribus Græcis tractata est, an quid et quantum inter Pyrrhonios et Academicos philosophos intersit[1]." After some remarks that give us less information than one would have anticipated, he comes to the conclusion that their opinions were pretty nearly identical. Lucian shared the opinion (Icar. 206), and is corrected by the Scholiast who observes, ἀντιδιαστέλλονται γὰρ τούτοις (sc. the Pyrrhoneans) οἱ ἐξ Ἀκαδημίας.

The discussion has been continued in modern times: most writers of the last century (Bayle notably) regarding the two schools as identical; in this century however the opposite opinion has prevailed. M. Thorbecke has argued at some length for a difference[2], and somewhat similar views have been adopted by Hegel and Zeller[3].

It is better not to confine the enquiry to the differences that Sextus would establish between his own school and the New Academy, but to take it in

[1] A. Gellius, *N. A.* x. 5.
[2] *Annales Acad. Lugd. Bat.* Vol. 5.
[3] Brandis appears to regard the difference as very small.

a wider form and compare the two theories in

1. Origin.
2. Aim.
3. Method.

Pyrrho lived at a time, when the warning words of the Platonic Socrates were peculiarly applicable. "Let us beware," he says[1], "of turning misologists as men turn misanthropists, for a man cannot fall a victim to a greater evil than misology. Misology and misanthropy come to pass in the same fashion. For a man assumes misanthropy after he has trusted some one without limit and without heed, supposing him to be at all times truly sound-hearted and trustworthy: shortly afterwards he finds this man, and subsequently another to be a scoundrel and a traitor. Whensoever this has befallen a man frequently, and more especially at the hands of those whom he supposed to be his nearest and dearest friends, from constant chagrin he begins to loathe all men and to suppose that there is nothing that is not rotten." If this caution was at all appropriate to the age of Plato, it was far more appropriate to that of Pyrrho; for Pyrrho's was an age of misology, and Pyrrho the most thorough-going misologist of the age.

The intellect of Greece was suffering from that depression which always follows a period of great

---

[1] Plat. *Phæd.* 89 D.

speculative activity: it had carried philosophy to a height never before attained: it sank back in doubt whether there be any truth in philosophy. The same problems had been discussed and re-discussed in manifold shapes and forms, and the solution was to all appearance as far distant as ever. Such a period of depression prevailed between the decay of Scholasticism and Descartes, between Wolf and the publication of the *Critique of Pure Reason*. But in Greece the depression was, as I have already endeavoured to show, heightened by the fall of Greek liberties and the declining vigour of the Greek mind. The former cause needs no further mention here. In earlier days, when the Greek mind was in the full maturity of power, doubt had assumed no unhealthy form. Aristotle remarks with an antithetical vigour which no translation can give: "ἔστι δὲ τοῖς εὐπορῆσαι βουλομένοις προὔργου τὸ διαπορῆσαι καλῶς¹:" but scepticism so hopeless and so complete as the Pyrrhonean was unknown to him, except as the reductio ad absurdum, to which the nihilism of some sceptics ought logically to lead; for Pyrrhonism is more thorough-going than any "Aufklärung." Imperfectly as the scheme was at first worked out, for all new schemes in their infancy must "stammer²," it was not an attack on this or that philosophy: it was the offspring of despair, and its verdict was a complete

---

[1] *Metaph.* II. 1, 2.   [2] Ar. *Metaph.* I. 10, 2.

abnegation of enquiry. Now the New Academy sprang from very different causes. In the first place, it came into being some fifty years later; and in a country like Greece, whose whole history as the home of an independent nation was so short, fifty years were a long period and saw many changes. Political circumstances had almost no influence in speculation, for the old union of speculation and action had passed away. Athens had become a cypher in the contests of kingdoms and nations: but more than ever was it the centre of the philosophical activity. The downfall of the small republics and the roving habits which the wide extension of *Hellas* had created, had made philosophers philosophers by profession without any tie of kindred or country. The philosophers of Athens were but seldom Athenians: not always Greeks. Take the Stoics, the least sophistic of all: Zeno of Citium, Cleanthes of Assos, Herillus of Carthage, Ariston of Chios, &c. It is not surprising that among men so situated the sophistic tendency became strong again, and of this tendency Arcesilas was in his day the most illustrious representative. The revolution in the course of philosophy which found its expression more especially in Zeno was in process of fulfilment, and his scepticism is by no means the result of despair. It is true that the Stoic and Epicurean systems were far narrower and more confined in their range than the Platonic and Aristotelian, and that they were individualistic to a degree that was logically fatal to coherence, but they were still in their youth, and, even if the old confidence was wanting, there was a renewed belief in the possibility of attaining knowledge. As I have already endeavoured to show, Arcesilas was led by a concurrence of causes to assault the Stoics: he does not seem to have been led to it by any profound conviction: he attacked a rival school with the weapons he borrowed from Pyrrho, not because he believed in the impossibility of knowledge, but because he believed Pyrrhonism to be the best means of refuting a dogmatic theory; he made use of Pyrrhonism as he might have used "the reaper" or any other of the fallacies which were so highly esteemed in that controversial age. Carneades, a more earnest and a profounder thinker, did not content himself with a bare negative: the care he took in building up and enlarging his doctrine of probability indicates that he considered a negative an unsatisfactory position. He did not see his way to a downright "yes," but he shrank from a complete "no." The view he took of the province of philosophy will be more conveniently discussed when we come to speak of the method of the Academy: suffice it to say that though he was probably more thoroughly convinced than Arcesilas of the limited power of the human faculties, he was far from adopting the Pyrrhonean stand-point, and the wide difference between them was recognized by the indirect as well as by the direct testimony of antiquity. The Pyrrhonists were always regarded as the foes of philosophy: the Academics were never suspected of abandoning philosophy. They were indeed accused by the Stoics of sapping the true grounds of morality, by the Epicureans of putting forward a rule of life, that was poor in theory and impossible in practice, but these were only the accusations of sects, who at least supposed that there was some ground held in common by themselves and their opponents. Nor did the Academics themselves knowingly deny philosophy. Cicero, who professed to be a disciple of Carneades, had no idea that he was not as much a student of philosophy, and a believer in its possibility as Cato or Balbus. Somewhat forgetful apparently of the way Arcesilas had appropriated the Pyrrhonean method, he classes Pyrrhonism and the doctrines of Herillus together as long-exploded heresies; and Seneca, while he recognizes the Zew Academy as a philosophical sect, exclaims: "Quis est qui tradat præcepta Pyrrhonis?"

As regards the summum bonum, the Pyrrhonists were in harmony with their age, the difference between them, the Stoics, and the Epicureans being more apparent than real; the aim of the Pyrrhonists was ἀταραξία, to be attained by means of ἐποχή. This ἀταραξία they allowed could only be attained to in certain matters: in those which they called "necessary" they were obliged to obey phenomena and practise μετριοπάθεια: such at least was their doctrine in later times: to them, as to the other schools of their time, philosophy was only a means to happiness. The one party sought knowledge in order to obtain it: with the very same end in view the other enforced ignorance. In this point on the other hand the Academy stood alone: Carneades (for the opinions of Arcesilas in this matter we know too imperfectly to speak of them with any confidence) did not disregard that connection with practical life which ran through the philosophy of the time. But in his time, a hundred years after the death of Zeno, men were far less confident than they had been, that a very strictly defined course of life would give them the result they longed for. Every species of end, it seemed, had been proposed, and it was not felt that any of these ends had conferred the anticipated benefits. Strict conformity to the letter had betrayed all sects into extravagance, and Carneades was only acting in accordance with his own principles and the feelings of the time, when he declined to make any particular choice. He thus gave his own school the enormous advantage, that his moral philosophy was essentially popular, a philosophy of the *juste milieu*, which avoided both the asceticism of the Stoics and the cold quiet of the Pyrrhonists, a quiet that had in it far more that was attractive to the Oriental than the Greek, and that never, as far as we know, found an ardent disciple to carry its διάθεσις into practice.

The practical teaching of the Academy was the echo of a prevailing sentiment: it was marked by good sense rather than profound insight, good feeling rather than profound principles.

When we come to consider the methods of the two schools, it is somewhat difficult to institute a comparison. The history of the New Academy is short. It arose, developed and flourished under much the same influences: it began and ended in Athens; for its Roman supporters are not sufficiently important to detain us here. Pyrrhonism began in republican Elis, when Greek liberty was passing away. After the death of Timon it ceased to attract disciples or defenders, and unhonoured and unnoticed during nearly four hundred years, it was revived under the Roman Empire, in circumstances that had little in common with those amidst which it began. It could not be expected that the later disciples should adhere without important deviations to a system which was so far removed from them. But these deviations can only be important in so far as they illustrate the teaching of Pyrrho: what was engrafted upon that, by borrowing from the Academy, must as a matter of course be restored to the source from which it was taken. When that is done, it is surprising how little in the bulky works of Sextus is suited to our purpose. The truth is, that Scepticism has not many principles. It is their application which forms at once its strength and its complexities, and the application of Pyrrhonism was first made by the New Academy and not by the Pyrrhonists. The three questions proposed by Pyrrho contained the kernel of the doctrine: the answer to the first question was that we have no knowledge of Things as they are in themselves, an answer quite in accordance with the general drift of the post-Aristotelian philosophy. The Absolute being thus destroyed, it only remained for the Pyrrhoneans to destroy the Relative, and it was to this end that their method was directed. This hostility to the Relative dominated, as we have frequently seen, in the whole of their polemic, and placed them in that position of unqualified scepticism, in which they seem to have taken an almost childish delight, using phrase after phrase to express the attitude they regarded as so admirable. We find even Ænesidemus declaring "that none of them (sc. the Pyrrhoneans) has said at all that all things are incomprehensible or comprehensible, and no more that they are such or such, at one time such and at another time not such, or to one such to another not such, to another not existent at all," and a good deal more in the same strain. It is very curious that they were not more conscious of the suicidal effect of their own method. Aristocles points it out, and it had doubtless been remarked by others, for Sextus makes a lame and unsatisfactory attempt to show that he was not a dogmatist. Pyrrhonism must not be confounded with other Scepticisms, and it is not fair to shelter it by an appeal to other thinkers, whose premises were very different, even if their methods were somewhat analogous. It was quite open to Hume for instance, to maintain that he could question the reasons of our belief in an external world, and yet believe in its existence. "We may well ask," he remarks, "what causes induce us to believe in the existence of body, but 'tis vain to ask whether there is body or not? that is a point which we must take for granted in all reasonings[1]." The Pyrrhonists however did not take this for granted: they denied that we can know whether there be body or not, and had no proper ground for admitting of the compulsion of phenomena. In fact they only stopped short when the absurdity of their position was shown by their application of it to practical life: but their arbitrary attempt to cut the knot by admitting a criterion in practice and excluding it in theory cannot be accepted. There are limits to Scepticism if it does not wish to destroy itself. It was quite legitimate for Ænesidemus to question the doctrine of Causality, but it was the reverse of legitimate to try to upset the doctrine of probation. Here we see the distinction between the Academy and the Pyrrhonists. Carneades and Cleitomachus were fond of using Logic for negative ends, yet they did not dream of denying Logic itself. The Sceptics do not appear to have seen that their supposed disproof of reasoning, if

---

[1] *Human Nature*, Part IV. § 1.

valid, disproved their own reasonings, if indeed we can allow those who did not allow of proof to talk of disproof. Sextus had a perfect right to pick to pieces the Stoic system of Logic, which he does with considerable skill. As he remarks, the Stoics confounded Concepts and Definitions together. The object defined is not apprehended from the Definition as the Stoic supposed, but the Concept is anterior to the Definition; and speaking of the absurd value the Stoics attach to definition, Sextus well asks, why people do not talk in definitions if they add so much to our information[1]. He rightly points out that a Concept, which is a species, cannot be co-extensive with the Concept, which is its genus. Even when he assails the validity of the syllogism as a form, he is not going beyond what is admissible and has been sanctioned by many eminent names.

No amount of ingenuity in particulars can however atone for the inadequate conception the Pyrrhoneans formed of philosophy. Had they laid hold of the critical method adopted by Ænesidemus in his eight tropes, they would have performed an inestimable service. This was an achievement greatly beyond what could be expected, and how far Ænesidemus was before his followers, when he attained, although in this instance, only, to the critical instead of the sceptical method, is shown by the signal manner in

[1] *P. H.* II. 207, 212.

which Sextus misunderstands the tropes. But it was not merely of an error of omission so venial as this that the Pyrrhoneans were guilty: they are open to a much graver charge. With all their ability and acuteness, and they possessed both in a large measure, they never comprehended the effects of their own work as a whole, or rose above the notion of attempting the subversion of all established principles. It is curious to observe how complacently Sextus remarks on the tendency of such an endeavour; and apparently believes that, because he professes to be dealing only with phenomena, he is quite safe in cutting away the ground on which he himself stands[1]. The New Academy on the other hand seems to me to have differed from the Pyrrhoneans most clearly, and especially in this point, that it did form a conception of philosophy as a whole. It regarded, I believe, the task of philosophy as purely formal—the classification of the representations made on the mind. The Pyrrhonean never allowed of anything beyond the "*Vorstellung*": Carneades forms the "*Begriff*" from the "*Vorstellung*"; and philosophy is in his estimation concerned not in the enlargement, strictly so speaking, of our knowledge, but in the arrangement of concepts. In short to the Academy as to Herbart philosophy is a "Bearbeitung der Begriffe," although of course the Herbartian philosophy is widely different from that of

---

[1] *Adv. Math.* VII. 361.

the Academy. I am aware that this view of the teaching of the Academy has not been much dwelt upon, but on the whole it seems to me to give the best explanation of the position of the School. Nor am I attributing this view of the formal character of philosophy to the Academy without authority: it is given by Cicero[1] to Philo, and I have at page 46 followed Zeller in ascribing it to Carneades. From what is known of Philo, one has little hesitation in regarding it as not peculiar to him, provided it suits the general teaching of the Academy. We have already seen that Carneades despaired of attaining to any certainty by physical investigations. There may be an Antipodes, the moon may be inhabited alone of the planetary bodies, the earth may be in motion: but he maintains, we have no means adequate to the solution of these questions. Again, we find both him and Arcesilas dwelling on the uncertainty of knowledge derived through the senses, and Carneades rejecting that also which is derived through what the Stoics termed the concepts of the Understanding. In conjunction with this, one must consider the dislike Arcesilas expressed for the Megarean Eristic, his depreciation of Dialectic[2], and the saying of Carneades, that Dialectic was like a polypus that devoured its own limbs[3]. At first all might lead us to class the Academy along with Pyrrho, and to believe that they both agreed in re-

---

[1] *Acad. Quaest.* II. 28. 91. [2] Stob. *Floril.* LXXXII. 4.
[3] *Ib.* LXXXII. 13. Cf. *Ib.* 14, in regard to Cleitomachus.

nouncing philosophy: especially would this be the case when we read the remarks of Carneades on the results derived from the reason, on the number of different sects, and the great problems which have been discussed and rediscussed, but which remain unsettled. This may be looked upon as an argument from despair, and indeed occurs several times in Sextus. Yet further reflection shows that it would be very extraordinary, if one so fond of controversy as Arcesilas, and who trained his pupils with a view to it, were altogether opposed to Eristic, if Carneades the renowned disputant, with whom few ventured to cross swords ("*digladiari*," Cic. ap. Nonium. p. 65), altogether abandoned Dialectic, or, for the remembrance of Pyrrho's fame in disputation might reconcile us to that, if Cleitomachus, who was by some called the founder of Dialectic philosophy, held such an opinion.

The solution of the difficulty is, I think, to be found in the Theory of Probability. I am not disposed to follow those who would identify the probable of the Academy with the Pyrrhonean phenomenon: the former is a much more scientific conception. It seems to me that in it lies, according to the Academy, the task of philosophy as a formal science: it is the supposed abuse only of Eristic and Dialectic that Arcesilas and Carneades would condemn, the attempt to make them a means of discovering the True: on the contrary, they regard the method of philosophy as a method of testing and classifying the concepts formed from the representations made to the mind: we cannot expect to reach to certainty: we can but register and compare concepts according to the standard of probability. It is easy to see that this doctrine is somewhat sterile and barren of result, but as a scientific Theory it is superior to Pyrrhonism, which with all its subtlety only rushes into a *reductio ad absurdum*. It is a pity that we do not know more of the constructive side of the philosophy of Carneades, for we do not exactly know how he established the Probable as a criterion while he denied the existence of Truth from the side of the Subjective. His destructive criticism has tended to obscure the other features of his system.

Thus, Pyrrhonists, allowing of no criterion and regarding every argument as equally true and equally false, arrived at results as fatal to themselves as to the dogmatists: the Academy, which had begun with the Socratic profession and the Socratic mode of examination, and employed the Pyrrhonean method merely as serviceable in assailing the Stoics and all who claimed absolute certitude, endeavoured, in Hume's language, "to resolve knowledge into probability." The accusation made by Sextus, that they dogmatically denied the possibility of knowledge, is untrue: perhaps their greatest error was their too ready adoption of the Pyrrhonean method, which inevitably led to consequences which they did not foresee, and would not have endorsed, and in their not seeing that the reasonings, used to support an alleged fact, are often false, while the fact alleged is true. Here lay the merit of Hume, whose scepticism is far more formidable to the experiential philosophers than theirs, and with whom they had much in common. What enhances the similarity is, that among the schools of the time they least of all regarded speculation as a means to an end. The Pyrrhonists were in this point at one with the Stoics and Epicureans: they professed absolute doubt only in order to arrive at undisturbed happiness. Carneades professed a moderated doubt and fixed upon no good as the highest, though his philosophy has throughout a reference to the Conduct of Life. It avoids that unattainable ideal which Pyrrhonism strove after, an ideal that though consonant to the tendencies of Pyrrho's age, seems to have little attraction for those who subsequently revived his doctrines. They indeed still proclaimed ἀταραξία as the end they sought for, though in this respect they were abandoned by Ænesidemus their greatest thinker, and the idea of undisturbed quiet in all probability won them but few disciples. From the number of physicians in their ranks one may believe that in the disorganized and unscientific state in which medicine was during the time immediately preceding Galen, the Pyrrhonean doubt appeared the only result practicable to the Empiric of the early empire. Sextus, however, belonged to the Methodici, and has tried to shew that the spirit of Pyrrhonism was antagonistic to the doctrines he himself opposed. Still he does not bring forward any grounds sufficient to upset the likelihood of a connection between the scepticism produced by the failure of philosophy and the failure of medicine[1].

From the late date at which both the Academy and the Pyrrhonists arose, they produced no dogmatic reaction. In an age when speculation was more vigorous, some one would probably have been stimulated to construct dogmatism anew in a more critical fashion, but the highest result they caused was the Stoicism of Chrysippus, which, in its turn, stimulated the ingenuity of Carneades. Their best efforts—the theories of Carneades and the critique of Causality and the eight Tropes of Ænesidemus—provoked no adequate response. The Neo-Platonists went back to Plato and Aristotle, and did not heed the revived doubt of their own day or the earlier polemic of the New Academy, but scepticism at least in the form given to it by Carneades still possessed much unobserved influence on those who had not joined either of what we may perhaps term the two rival camps of Neo-Platonism and Christianity. We may conjecture this from what St Augustine says in his Retractations, and from the dialogue he wrote against the Academy, in which he discusses with his friends, Alypius, Licen-

[1] If this is correct, it is an additional reason in favour of the late date of Ænesidemus.

tius and Trigetius, the same problems that Cicero discusses with Lucullus. We find too St Gregory of Nazianzus complaining of the troubles and confusions since "the Sexti and Pyrrhoneans and the spirit of contradiction were perniciously intruded into our churches like some evil and malignant plague." But the constructive tendencies of the age prevailed, and the whole philosophical energy of the fourth and fifth centuries were devoted to aims other than sceptical. It is curious however to observe that, when the revolt against authority, which marked the 16th and 17th centuries, brought scepticism in its train, while the Roman Church clung to Scholasticism and the Protestants to Aristotle, an attempt was made to found modern Scepticism on the old. Foucher wrote a history of the New Academy and Sorbière translated the Hypotheses of Sextus: yet it is not in these imitators, but in Pascal and Hume, with all their likeness and all their unlikeness, that we must look for the true successors of Pyrrho and Carneades.

December, 1868.

16, BEDFORD STREET, COVENT GARDEN, LONDON.

MACMILLAN AND CO.'S
List of Publications.

Æschyli Eumenides.
 The Greek Text with English Notes, and an Introduction. By BERNARD DRAKE, M.A. 8vo. 7s. 6d.

AIRY.—*Works by* G. B. AIRY, M.A. LL.D. D.C.L. *Astronomer Royal, &c.*

 Treatise on the Algebraical and Numerical Theory of Errors of Observations and the Combination of Observations.
  Crown 8vo. 6s. 6d.

 Popular Astronomy.
  A Series of Lectures delivered at Ipswich. 18mo. cloth, 4s. 6d. With Illustrations. Uniform with MACMILLAN'S SCHOOL CLASS BOOKS.

 An Elementary Treatise on Partial Differential Equations.
  With Stereoscopic Cards of Diagrams. Crown 8vo. 5s. 6d.

 On the Undulatory Theory of Optics.
  Designed for the use of Students in the University. Crown 8vo. 6s. 6d.

 On Sound and Atmospheric Vibrations,
  With the Mathematical Elements of Music. Designed for the use of Students of the Universities. Crown 8vo. 9s.

Algebraical Exercises.
 Progressively arranged by Rev. C. A. JONES, M.A. and C. H. CHEYNE, M.A. Mathematical Masters in Westminster School. 18mo. 2s. 6d.

A

Alice's Adventures in Wonderland.
>By LEWIS CARROLL. With Forty-two Illustrations by TENNIEL. 14th Thousand. Crown 8vo. cloth. 6s.

ALLINGHAM.—*Laurence Bloomfield in Ireland.*
>A Modern Poem. By WILLIAM ALLINGHAM. Fcap. 8vo. 7s.

ANSTED.—*The Great Stone Book of Nature.*
>By DAVID THOMAS ANSTED, M.A. F.R.S. F.G.S. Fcap. 8vo. 5s.

ANSTIE.—*Stimulants and Narcotics, their Mutual Relations.*
>With Special Researches on the Action of Alcohol, Æther, and Chloroform on the Vital Organism. By FRANCIS E. ANSTIE, M.D. M.R.C.P. 8vo. 14s.

Neuralgia, and Diseases which resemble it.
>8vo. [In the Press.

Aristotle on Fallacies; or, the Sophistici Elenchi.
>With a Translation and Notes by EDWARD POSTE, M.A. 8vo. 8s. 6d.

ARNOLD.—*Works by* MATTHEW ARNOLD.
>*New Poems. Second Edition.*
>>Extra fcap. 8vo. 6s. 6d.

>*A French Eton; or, Middle-Class Education and the State.*
>>Fcap. 8vo. 2s. 6d.

>*Essays in Criticism.*
>>New Edition. Extra fcap. 8vo. 6s.

>*Schools and Universities on the Continent.*
>>8vo. 10s. 6d.

BAKER.—*Works by* SIR SAMUEL W. BAKER, M.A. F.R.G.S.
>*The Nile Tributaries of Abyssinia, and the Sword Hunters of the Hamran Arabs.*
>>With Portraits, Maps, and Illustrations. *Third Edition.* 8vo. 21s.

>*The Albert N'yanza Great Basin of the Nile, and Exploration of the Nile Sources. New and cheaper Edition.*
>>With Portraits, Maps, and Illustrations. Two Vols. crown 8vo. 16s.

>*Cast up by the Sea; or, The Adventures of Ned Grey.*
>>With Illustrations. Crown 8vo.

BARWELL.—*Guide in the Sick Room.*
>By RICHARD BARWELL, F.R.C.S. Extra fcap. 8vo. 3s. 6d.

BARNES.—*Poems of Rural Life in Common English.*
  By the Rev. W. BARNES, Author of " Poems of Rural Life in the Dorset Dialect." Fcap. 8vo. 6s.

BATES AND LOCKYER.—*A Class-Book of Geography. Adapted to the recent programme of the Royal Geographical Society.*
  By H. W. BATES and J. N. LOCKYER, F.R.G.S. [In the Press.

BAXTER.—*National Income.*
  By R. DUDLEY BAXTER, M.A. With Coloured Diagram. 8vo. 3s. 6d.

BAYMA.—*Elements of Molecular Mechanics.*
  By JOSEPH BAYMA, S. J. 8vo. 10s. 6d.

BEASLEY.—*An Elementary Treatise on Plane Trigonometry.*
  With a Numerous Collection of Examples. By R. D. BEASLEY, M.A. Second Edition. Crown 8vo. 3s. 6d.

BELL.—*Romances and Minor Poems.*
  By HENRY GLASSFORD BELL. Fcap. 8vo. 6s.

BERNARD.—*The Progress of Doctrine in the New Testament.*
  In Eight Lectures preached before the University of Oxford. By THOMAS DEHANY BERNARD, M.A. Second Edition. 8vo. 8s. 6d.

BERNARD.—*Four Lectures on Subjects connected with Diplomacy.*
  By MOUNTAGUE BERNARD, M.A., Chichele Professor of International Law and Diplomacy, Oxford. 8vo. 9s.

BERNARD (ST.).—*The Life and Times of St. Bernard, Abbot of Clairvaux.*
  By J. C. MORISON, M.A. *New Edition.* Crown 8vo. 7s. 6d.

BESANT.—*Studies in Early French Poetry.*
  By WALTER BESANT, M.A. Crown 8vo. 8s. 6d.

BIRKS.—*Works by* THOMAS RAWSON BIRKS, M.A.
  The Difficulties of Belief in connexion with the Creation and the Fall.
    Crown 8vo. 4s. 6d.
  On Matter and Ether ; or, the Secret Laws of Physical Change.
    Crown 8vo. 5s. 6d.

BLAKE.—*The Life of William Blake, the Artist.*
  By ALEXANDER GILCHRIST. With numerous Illustrations from Blake's Designs and Fac-similes of his Studies of the "Book of Job." Two Vols. Medium 8vo. 32s.

BLAKE.—*A Visit to some American Schools and Colleges.*
  By SOPHIA JEX BLAKE. Crown 8vo. 6s.

Blanche Lisle, and other Poems.
  By CECIL HOME. Fcap. 8vo. 4s. 6d.

BOOLE.—*Works by the late* GEORGE BOOLE, F.R.S. *Professor of Mathematics in the Queen's University, Ireland, &c.*

  A Treatise on Differential Equations.
    New Edition. Edited by I. TODHUNTER, M.A. F.R.S. Crown 8vo. 14s.

  Treatise on Differential Equations.
    Supplementary Volume. Crown 8vo. 8s. 6d.

  A Treatise on the Calculus of Finite Differences.
    Crown 8vo. 10s. 6d.

BRADSHAW.—*An Attempt to ascertain the state of Chaucer's Works, as they were Left at his Death,*
  With some Notices of their Subsequent History. By HENRY BRADSHAW, of King's College, and the University Library, Cambridge. [In the Press.

BRIGHT.—*Speeches on various Questions of Public Policy.*
  By JOHN BRIGHT, M.P. Edited by PROFESSOR THOROLD ROGERS. 2 vols. 8vo. 25s.

BRIMLEY.—*Essays by the late* GEORGE BRIMLEY, M.A.
  Edited by W. G. CLARK, M.A. With Portrait. *Cheaper Edition.* Fcap. 8vo. 3s. 6d.

BROOK SMITH.—*Arithmetic in Theory and Practice.*
  For Advanced Pupils. Part First. By J. BROOK SMITH, M.A. Crown 8vo. 3s. 6d.

BRYCE.—*The Holy Roman Empire.*
  By JAMES BRYCE, B.C.L. Fellow of Oriel College, Oxford. *A New Edition, revised and enlarged.* Crown 8vo. 9s.

BUCKNILL.—*The Mad Folk of Shakespeare.*
  Psychological Lectures by J. C. BUCKNILL, M.D. F.R.S. Second Edition. Crown 8vo. 6s. 6d.

BULLOCK.—*Works by* W. H. BULLOCK.
> *Polish Experiences during the Insurrection of* 1863-4.
> Crown 8vo. With Map. 8s. 6d.
>
> *Across Mexico in* 1864-5.
> With Coloured Map and Illustrations. Crown 8vo. 10s. 6d.

BURGON.—*A Treatise on the Pastoral Office.*
> Addressed chiefly to Candidates for Holy Orders, or to those who have recently undertaken the cure of souls. By the Rev. JOHN W. BURGON, M.A. 8vo. 12s.

BUTLER (ARCHER).—*Works by the Rev.* WILLIAM ARCHER BUTLER, M.A. *late Professor of Moral Philosophy in the University of Dublin.*
> *Sermons, Doctrinal and Practical.*
> Edited, with a Memoir of the Author's Life, by THOMAS WOODWARD, M.A. Dean of Down. With Portrait. *Seventh and Cheaper Edition.* 8vo. 8s.
>
> *A Second Series of Sermons.*
> Edited by J. A. JEREMIE, D.D. Regius Professor of Divinity at Cambridge. *Fifth and Cheaper Edition.* 8vo. 7s.
>
> *History of Ancient Philosophy.*
> Edited by WM. H. THOMPSON, M.A. Master of Trinity College, Cambridge. Two Vols. 8vo. 1l. 5s.
>
> *Letters on Romanism, in reply to Dr. Newman's Essay on Development.*
> Edited by the Dean of Down. *Second Edition*, revised by Archdeacon HARDWICK. 8vo. 10s. 6d.

BUTLER (MONTAGU).—*Sermons preached in the Chapel of Harrow School.*
> By H. MONTAGU BUTLER, Head Master. Crown 8vo. 7s. 6d.

BUTLER (GEORGE).—*Works by the Rev.* GEORGE BUTLER.
> *Family Prayers.*
> Crown 8vo. 5s.
>
> *Sermons preached in Cheltenham College Chapel.*
> Crown 8vo. 7s. 6d.

CAIRNES.—*The Slave Power; its Character, Career, and Probable Designs.*
> Being an Attempt to Explain the Real Issues Involved in the American Contest. By J. E. CAIRNES, M.A. *Second Edition.* 8vo. 10s. 6d.

CALDERWOOD.—*Philosophy of the Infinite.*
A Treatise on Man's Knowledge of the Infinite Being, in answer to Sir W. Hamilton and Dr. Mansel. By the Rev. HENRY CALDERWOOD, M.A. Professor of Moral Philosophy at Edinburgh. *Second Edition.* 8vo. 14s.

Cambridge Senate-House Problems and Riders, with Solutions.

1848—1851.—*Problems.*
By FERRERS and JACKSON. 15s. 6d.

1848—1851.—*Riders.*
By JAMESON. 7s. 6d.

1854.—*Problems and Riders.*
By WALTON and MACKENZIE, M.A. 10s. 6d.

1857.—*Problems and Riders.*
By CAMPION and WALTON. 8s. 6d.

1860.—*Problems and Riders.*
By WATSON and ROUTH. 7s. 6d.

1864.—*Problems and Riders.*
By WALTON and WILKINSON. 10s. 6d.

Cambridge Lent Sermons.—
Sermons preached during Lent, 1864, in Great St. Mary's Church, Cambridge. By the BISHOP of OXFORD, Rev. H. P. LIDDON, T. L. CLAUGHTON, J. R. WOODFORD, Dr. GOULBURN, J. W. BURGON, T. T. CARTER, Dr. PUSEY, DEAN HOOK, W. J. BUTLER, DEAN GOODWIN. Crown 8vo. 7s. 6d.

Cambridge Course of Elementary Natural Philosophy, for the Degree of B.A.
Originally compiled by J. C. SNOWBALL, M.A., late Fellow of St. John's College. *Fifth Edition,* revised and enlarged, and adapted for the Middle-Class Examinations by THOMAS LUND, B.D. Crown 8vo. 5s.

Cambridge and Dublin Mathematical Journal.
The Complete Work, in Nine Vols. 8vo. Cloth. 7l. 4s. Only a few copies remain on hand.

Cambridge Characteristics in the Seventeenth Century.
By JAMES BASS MULLINGER, B.A. Crown 8vo. 4s. 6d.

CAMPBELL.—*Works by* JOHN M'LEOD CAMPBELL.
 Thoughts on Revelation, with Special Reference to the Present Time.
  Crown 8vo. 5s.
 The Nature of the Atonement, and its Relation to Remission of Sins and Eternal Life.
  Third Edition. With an Introduction and Notes. 8vo. 10s. 6d.

CARTER.—*King's College Chapel: Notes on its History and present condition.*
  By T. J. P. CARTER, M.A. Fellow of King's College, Cambridge. With Photographs. 8vo. 5s.

Catullus.
  Edited by R. ELLIS. 18mo. 3s. 6d.

CHALLIS.—*Creation in Plan and in Progress:*
  Being an Essay on the First Chapter of Genesis. By the Rev. JAMES CHALLIS, M.A. F.R.S. F.R.A.S. Crown 8vo. 3s. 6d.

CHATTERTON.—*Leonore; a Tale.*
  By GEORGIANA LADY CHATTERTON. *A New Edition.* Beautifully printed on thick toned paper. Crown 8vo. with Frontispiece and Vignette Title engraved by JEENS. 7s. 6d.

CHEYNE.—*Works by* C. H. H. CHEYNE, B.A.
 An Elementary Treatise on the Planetary Theory.
  With a Collection of Problems. Crown 8vo. 6s. 6d.
 The Earth's Motion of Rotation (including the Theory of Precession and Nutation).
  Crown 8vo. 3s. 6d.

Choice Notes on St. Matthew, drawn from Old and New Sources.
  Crown 8vo. 4s. 6d.

CHRISTIE (J. R.).—*Elementary Test Questions in Pure and Mixed Mathematics.*
  Crown 8vo. 8s. 6d.

Church Congress (Authorized Report of) held at Wolverhampton in October, 1867.
  8vo. 3s. 6d.

CHURCH.—*Sermons preached before the University of Oxford.*
  By R. W. CHURCH, M.A. late Fellow of Oriel College, Rector of Whatley. Extra fcap. 8vo. 4s. 6d.

CICERO.—*The Second Philippic Oration.*
> With an Introduction and Notes, translated from KARL HALM. Edited, with Corrections and Additions, by JOHN E. B. MAYOR, M.A. *Third Edition.* Fcap. 8vo. 5s.

CLARK.—*Four Sermons preached in the Chapel of Trinity College, Cambridge.*
> By W. G. CLARK, M.A. Fcap. 8vo. 2s. 6d.

CLAY.—*The Prison Chaplain.*
> A Memoir of the Rev. JOHN CLAY, B.D. late Chaplain of the Preston Goal. With Selections from his Reports and Correspondence, and a Sketch of Prison Discipline in England. By his Son, the Rev. W. L. CLAY, M.A. 8vo. 15s.

The Power of the Keys.
> Sermons preached in Coventry. By the Rev. W. L. CLAY, M.A. Fcap. 8vo. 3s. 6d.

Clergyman's Self-Examination concerning the Apostles' Creed.
> Extra fcap. 8vo. 1s. 6d.

CLOUGH.—*The Poems of Arthur Hugh Clough,*
> sometime Fellow of Oriel College, Oxford. With a Memoir by F. T. PALGRAVE. *Second Edition.* Fcap. 8vo. 6s.

COLENSO.—*Works by the Right Rev.* J. W. COLENSO, D.D. *Bishop of Natal.*

The Colony of Natal.
> A Journal of Visitation. With a Map and Illustrations. Fcap. 8vo. 5s.

Village Sermons.
> *Second Edition.* Fcap. 8vo. 2s. 6d.

Four Sermons on Ordination and on Missions.
> 18mo. 1s.

Companion to the Holy Communion,
> Containing the Service and Select Readings from the writings of Professor MAURICE. *Fine Edition* morocco, antique style, 6s. Common paper, 1s.

Letter to His Grace the Archbishop of Canterbury,
> Upon the Question of Polygamy, as found already existing in Converts from Heathenism. *Second Edition.* Crown 8vo. 1s. 6d.

Connells of Castle Connell.
> By JANET GORDON. Two Vols. Crown 8vo. 21s.

COOPER.—*Athenae Cantabrigienses.*
> By CHARLES HENRY COOPER, F.S.A. and THOMPSON COOPER, F.S.A. Vol. I. 8vo. 1500—85, 18s. Vol. II. 1586—1609, 18s.

LIST OF PUBLICATIONS.

COPE.—*An Introduction to Aristotle's Rhetoric.*
   With Analysis, Notes, and Appendices. By E. M. COPE, Senior Fellow and Tutor of Trinity College, Cambridge. 8vo. 14s.

COTTON.—*Works by the late* GEORGE EDWARD LYNCH COTTON, D.D. *Bishop of Calcutta.*

   Sermons and Addresses delivered in Marlborough College during Six Years.
   Crown 8vo. 10s. 6d.

   Sermons, chiefly connected with Public Events of 1854.
   Fcap. 8vo. 3s.

   Sermons preached to English Congregations in India.
   Crown 8vo. 7s. 6d.

   Expository Sermons on the Epistles for the Sundays of the Christian Year.
   Two Vols. Crown 8vo. 15s.

COX.—*Recollections of Oxford.*
   By G. V. Cox, M.A. late Esquire Bedel and Coroner in the University of Oxford. Crown 8vo. 10s. 6d.

CRAIK.—*My First Journal.*
   A Book for the Young. By GEORGIANA M. CRAIK, Author of "Riverston," "Lost and Won," &c. Royal 16mo. Cloth, gilt leaves, 3s. 6d.

CURE.—*The Seven Words of Christ on the Cross.*
   Sermons preached at St. George's, Bloomsbury. By the Rev. E. CAPEL CURE, M.A. Fcap. 8vo. 3s. 6d.

DALTON.—*Arithmetical Examples progressively arranged; together with Miscellaneous Exercises and Examination Papers.*
   By the Rev. T. DALTON, M.A. Assistant Master at Eton College. 18mo. 2s. 6d.

DANTE.—*Dante's Comedy, The Hell.*
   Translated by W. M. ROSSETTI. Fcap. 8vo. cloth. 5s.

DAVIES.—*Works by the Rev.* J. LLEWELYN DAVIES, M.A. *Rector of Christ Church, St. Marylebone, &c.*

   Sermons on the Manifestation of the Son of God.
   With a Preface addressed to Laymen on the present position of the Clergy of the Church of England; and an Appendix, on the Testimony of Scripture and the Church as to the Possibility of Pardon in the Future State. Fcap. 8vo. 6s. 6d.

DAVIES.—*The Work of Christ; or, the World Reconciled to God.*
With a Preface on the Atonement Controversy. Fcap. 8vo. 6s.

Baptism, Confirmation, and the Lord's Supper.
As interpreted by their outward signs. Three Expository Addresses for Parochial Use. Fcap. 8vo. Limp cloth. 1s. 6d.

Morality according to the Sacrament of the Lord's Supper.
Crown 8vo. 3s. 6d.

The Epistles of St. Paul to the Ephesians, the Colossians, and Philemon.
With Introductions and Notes, and an Essay on the Traces of Foreign Elements in the Theology of these Epistles. 8vo. 7s. 6d.

DAWSON.—*Acadian Geology, the Geological Structure, Organic Remains, and Mineral Resources of Nova Scotia, New Brunswick, and Prince Edward Island.*
By J. W. DAWSON, LL.D. F.R.S. F.G.S. Second Edition, revised and enlarged, with Geological Maps and Illustrations. 8vo. 18s.

DAY.—*Properties of Conic Sections proved Geometrically.*
By the Rev. H. G. DAY, M.A. Head-Master of Sedburgh Grammar School. Crown 8vo. 3s. 6d.

Days of Old; Stories from Old English History.
By the Author of "Ruth and her Friends." *New Edition*, 18mo. cloth, gilt leaves. 3s. 6d.

Demosthenes, De Corona.
The Greek Text with English Notes. By B. DRAKE, M.A. *Third Edition*, to which is prefixed ÆSCHINES AGAINST CTESIPHON, with English Notes. Fcap 8vo. 5s.

DE TEISSIER.—*Works by* G. F. DE TEISSIER, B.D.

Village Sermons.
Crown 8vo. 9s.

Second Series.
Crown 8vo. 8s. 6d.

The House of Prayer; or, a Practical Exposition of the Order for Morning and Evening Prayer in the Church of England.
18mo. extra cloth. 4s. 6d.

DE VERE.—*The Infant Bridal, and other Poems.*
By AUBREY DE VERE. Fcap. 8vo. 7s. 6d.

LIST OF PUBLICATIONS. 11

DILKE.—*Greater Britain.*
A Record of Travel in English-speaking Countries during 1866-7. (America, Australia, India.) By CHARLES WENTWORTH DILKE. Two Vols. 8vo. 28s.

DODGSON.—*Elementary Treatise on Determinants.*
By C. L. DODGSON, M.A. 4to. 10s. 6d.

DONALDSON.—*A Critical History of Christian Literature and Doctrine, from the Death of the Apostles to the Nicene Council.*
By JAMES DONALDSON, LL.D. Three Vols. 8vo. cloth. 31s.

DOYLE.—*The Return of the Guards, and other Poems.*
By Sir FRANCIS HASTINGS DOYLE, Professor of Poetry in the University of Oxford. Fcap. 8vo. 7s.

DREW.—*Works by W. H. DREW, M.A.*

A Geometrical Treatise on Conic Sections.
Third Edition. Crown 8vo. 4s. 6d.

Solutions to Problems contained in Drew's Treatise on Conic Sections.
Crown 8vo. 4s. 6d.

Early Egyptian History for the Young.
With Descriptions of the Tombs and Monuments. *New Edition*, with Frontispiece. Fcap. 8vo. 5s.

EASTWOOD.—*The Bible Word Book.*
A Glossary of Old English Bible Words. By J. EASTWOOD, M.A. of St. John's College, and W. ALDIS WRIGHT, M.A. Trinity College, Cambridge. 18mo. 5s. 6d. Uniform with Macmillan's School Class Books.

Ecce Homo.
A Survey of the Life and Work of Jesus Christ. 23d Thousand. Crown 8vo. 6s.

Echoes of Many Voices from Many Lands.
By A. F. 18mo. cloth, extra gilt. 3s. 6d.

ELLICE.—*English Idylls.*
By JANE ELLICE. Fcap. 8vo. cloth. 6s.

ELLIOTT.—*Life of Henry Venn Elliott, of Brighton.*
By JOSIAH BATEMAN, M.A. Author of "Life of Daniel Wilson, Bishop of Calcutta," &c. With Portrait, engraved by JEENS. Crown 8vo. 8s. 6d.

Essays on Church Policy.
Edited by the Rev. W. L. CLAY, M.A. Incumbent of Rainhill, Lancashire. 8vo. 9s.

Essays on a Liberal Education.
By Various Writers. Edited by the Rev. F. W. FARRAR, M.A. F.R.S. &c. Second Edition. 8vo. 10s. 6d.

EVANS.—*Brother Fabian's Manuscript, and other Poems.*
By SEBASTIAN EVANS. Fcap. 8vo. cloth. 6s.

FARRAR.—*The Fall of Man, and other Sermons.*
By the Rev. F. W. FARRAR, M.A. late Fellow of Trinity College, Cambridge. Fcap. 8vo. 6s.

FAWCETT.— *Works by* HENRY FAWCETT, M.P.
The Economic Position of the British Labourer.
Extra fcap. 8vo. 5s.
Manual of Political Economy.
Second Edition. Crown 8vo. 12s.

Fellowship: Letters addressed to my Sister Mourners.
Fcap. 8vo. cloth gilt. 3s. 6d.

FERRERS.—*A Treatise on Trilinear Co-ordinates, the Method of Reciprocal Polars, and the Theory of Projections.*
By the Rev. N. M. FERRERS, M.A. Second Edition. Crown 8vo. 6s. 6d.

FLETCHER.—*Thoughts from a Girl's Life.*
By LUCY FLETCHER. Second Edition. Fcap. 8vo. 4s. 6d.

FORBES.—*Life of Edward Forbes, F.R.S.*
By GEORGE WILSON, M.D. F.R.S.E., and ARCHIBALD GEIKIE, F.R.S. 8vo. with Portrait. 14s.

FORBES.—*The Voice of God in the Psalms.*
By GRANVILLE FORBES, Rector of Broughton. Crown 8vo. 6s. 6d.

FOX.—*On the Diagnosis and Treatment of the Varieties of Dyspepsia, considered in Relation to the Pathological Origin of the different Forms of Indigestion.*
By WILSON FOX, M.D. Lond. F.R.C.P. , Holme Professor of Clinical Medicine at University College, London, and Physician to University College Hospital. Second Edition. Demy 8vo. 7s. 6d.

On the Artificial Production of Tubercle in the Lower Animals.
4to. 5s. 6d.

FREELAND.—*The Fountain of Youth.*
> Translated from the Danish of Frederick Paludan Müller. By HUMPHREY WILLIAM FREELAND, late M.P. for Chichester. With Illustrations designed by Walter Allen. Crown 8vo. 6s.

FREEMAN.—*History of Federal Government from the Foundation of the Achaian League to the Disruption of the United States.*
> By EDWARD A. FREEMAN, M.A. Vol. 1. General Introduction.—History of the Greek Federations. 8vo. 21s.

FRENCH.—*Notes on the Characters in Shakespeare's Plays.*
> By G. R. FRENCH. [In the Press.

FROST.—*The First Three Sections of Newton's Principia.*
> With Notes and Problems in Illustration of the Subject By PERCIVAL FROST, M.A. *Second Edition.* 8vo. 10s. 6d.

FROST AND WOLSTENHOLME.—*A Treatise on Solid Geometry.*
> By the Rev. PERCIVAL FROST, M.A. and the Rev. J. WOLSTENHOLME, M.A. 8vo. 18s.

The Sicilian Expedition.
> Being Books VI. and VII. of Thucydides, with Notes. By the Rev. P. FROST, M.A. Fcap. 8vo. 5s.

FURNIVALL.—*Le Morte Arthur.*
> Edited from the Harleian M.S. 2252, in the British Museum. By F. J. FURNIVALL, M.A. With Essay by the late HERBERT COLERIDGE. Fcap. 8vo. 7s. 6d.

GALTON.—*Meteorographica, or Methods of Mapping the Weather.*
> Illustrated by upwards of 600 Printed Lithographed Diagrams. By FRANCIS GALTON, F.R.S. 4to. 9s.

GEIKIE.—*Works by* ARCHIBALD GEIKIE, F.R.S. *Director of the Geological Survey of Scotland.*

Story of a Boulder; or, Gleanings by a Field Geologist.
> Illustrated with Woodcuts. Crown 8vo. 5s.

Scenery of Scotland, viewed in connexion with its Physical Geology.
> With Illustrations and a New Geological Map. Crown 8vo. 10s. 6d.

Elementary Lessons in Physical Geology. [In the Press.

GIFFORD.—*The Glory of God in Man.*
> By E. H. GIFFORD, D.D. Fcap. 8vo. 3s. 6d.

Globe Editions :

The Complete Works of William Shakespeare.
Edited by W. G. CLARK and W. ALDIS WRIGHT. Ninety-first Thousand. Globe 8vo. 3s. 6d.; paper covers, 2s. 6d.

Morte DArthur.
SIR THOMAS MALORY'S Book of KING ARTHUR and of his noble KNIGHTS of the ROUND TABLE. The Edition of Caxton, revised for Modern use. With an Introduction by SIR EDWARD STRACHEY, Bart. Globe 8vo. 3s. 6d.

The Poetical Works of Sir Walter Scott.
With Biographical Essay by F. T. PALGRAVE.

The Poetical Works and Letters of Robert Burns.
Edited, with Life, by ALEXANDER SMITH. Globe 8vo. 3s. 6d.

The Adventures of Robinson Crusoe.
Edited, with Introduction, by HENRY KINGSLEY. Globe 8vo. 3s. 6d.

Goldsmith's Miscellaneous Works.
With Biographical Essay by PROF. MASSON. Globe 8vo. 3s. 6d.

Other Standard Works are in the Press.

Globe Atlas of Europe.
Uniform in Size with MACMILLAN'S GLOBE SERIES. Containing Forty-Eight Coloured Maps on the same scale, Plans of London and Paris, and a Copious Index. Strongly bound in half morocco, with flexible back, 9s.

GODFRAY.—*An Elementary Treatise on the Lunar Theory.*
With a brief Sketch of the Problem up to the time of Newton. By HUGH GODFRAY, M.A. *Second Edition revised.* Crown 8vo. 5s. 6d.

A Treatise on Astronomy, for the Use of Colleges and Schools.
By HUGH GODFRAY, M.A. 8vo. 12s. 6d.

Golden Treasury Series :
Uniformly printed in 18mo. with Vignette Titles by Sir NOEL PATON, T. WOOLNER, W. HOLMAN HUNT, J. E. MILLAIS, ARTHUR HUGHES, &c. Engraved on Steel by JEENS. Bound in extra cloth, 4s. 6d.; morocco plain, 7s. 6d.; morocco extra, 10s. 6d. each volume.

The Golden Treasury of the Best Songs and Lyrical Poems in the English Language.
Selected and arranged, with Notes, by FRANCIS TURNER PALGRAVE.

The Children's Garland from the Best Poets.
Selected and arranged by COVENTRY PATMORE.

Golden Treasury Series—continued.

The Book of Praise.
From the Best English Hymn Writers. Selected and arranged by Sir ROUNDELL PALMER. *A New and Enlarged Edition.*

The Fairy Book: the Best Popular Fairy Stories.
Selected and rendered anew by the Author of "John Halifax, Gentleman."

The Ballad Book.
A Selection of the choicest British Ballads. Edited by WILLIAM ALLINGHAM.

The Jest Book.
The choicest Anecdotes and Sayings. Selected and arranged by MARK LEMON.

Bacon's Essays and Colours of Good and Evil.
With Notes and Glossarial Index, by W. ALDIS WRIGHT, M.A.
*** Large paper copies, crown 8vo. 7s. 6d.; or bound in half morocco, 10s. 6d.

The Pilgrim's Progress
From this World to that which is to Come. By JOHN BUNYAN.
*** Large paper copies, crown 8vo. cloth, 7s. 6d.; or bound in half morocco, 10s. 6d.

The Sunday Book of Poetry for the Young.
Selected and arranged by C. F. ALEXANDER.

A Book of Golden Deeds of all Times and all Countries.
Gathered and Narrated anew by the Author of "The Heir of Redclyffe."

The Poetical Works of Robert Burns.
Edited, with Biographical Memoir, by ALEXANDER SMITH. Two Vols.

The Adventures of Robinson Crusoe.
Edited from the Original Editions by J. W. CLARK, M.A.

The Republic of Plato.
Translated into English with Notes by J. Ll. DAVIES, M.A. and D. J. VAUGHAN, M.A.

The Song Book.
Words and Tunes from the best Poets and Musicians, selected and arranged by JOHN HULLAH.

La Lyre Française.
Selected and arranged, with Notes, by GUSTAVE MASSON.

Tom Brown's School Days.
By an OLD BOY.

GREEN.—*Spiritual Philosophy.*
> Founded on the Teaching of the late SAMUEL TAYLOR COLERIDGE. By the late JOSEPH HENRY GREEN, F.R.S. D.C.L. Edited, with a Memoir of the Author's Life, by JOHN SIMON, F.R.S. Two Vols. 8vo. cloth. 25s.

Guesses at Truth.
> By Two BROTHERS. With Vignette Title and Frontispiece. *New Edition.* Fcap. 8vo. 6s.

GUIZOT, M.—*Memoir of M. de Barante.*
> Translated by the Author of "John Halifax, Gentleman." Crown 8vo. 6s. 6d.

Guide to the Unprotected
> In Every Day Matters relating to Property and Income. By a BANKER'S DAUGHTER. *Third Edition.* Extra fcap. 8vo. 3s. 6d.

HAMERTON.—*A Painter's Camp in the Highlands.*
> By P. G. HAMERTON. *New and Cheaper Edition,* one vol. Extra fcap. 8vo. 6s.

Etching and Etchers.
> A Treatise Critical and Practical. By P. G. HAMERTON. With Original Plates by REMBRANDT, CALLOT, DUJARDIN, PAUL POTTER, &c. Royal 8vo. Half morocco. 31s. 6d.

HAMILTON.—*On Truth and Error.*
> Thoughts on the Principles of Truth, and the Causes and Effect of Error. By JOHN HAMILTON. Crown 8vo. 5s.

HARDWICK.—*Works by the Ven.* ARCHDEACON HARDWICK.
Christ and other Masters.
> A Historical Inquiry into some of the Chief Parallelisms and Contrasts between Christianity and the Religious Systems of the Ancient World. *New Edition,* revised, and a Prefatory Memoir by the Rev. FRANCIS PROCTER. Two vols. crown 8vo. 15s.

A History of the Christian Church.
> Middle Age. From Gregory the Great to the Excommunication of Luther. Edited by FRANCIS PROCTER, M.A. With Four Maps constructed for this work by A. KEITH JOHNSTON. *Second Edition.* Crown 8vo. 10s. 6d.

A History of the Christian Church during the Reformation.
> Revised by FRANCIS PROCTER, M.A. *Second Edition.* Crown 8vo. 10s. 6d.

Twenty Sermons for Town Congregations.
> Crown 8vo. 6s. 6d.

HELPS.—*Realmah.*
> By ARTHUR HELPS. Two vols. crown 8vo. 16s.

LIST OF PUBLICATIONS.

HEMMING.—*An Elementary Treatise on the Differential and Integral Calculus.*
By G. W. HEMMING, M.A. *Second Edition.* 8vo. 9s.

HERSCHEL.—*The Iliad of Homer.*
Translated into English Hexameters. By Sir JOHN HERSCHEL, Bart. 8vo. 18s.

HERVEY.—*The Genealogies of our Lord and Saviour Jesus Christ,*
As contained in the Gospels of St. Matthew and St. Luke, reconciled with each other, and shown to be in harmony with the true Chronology of the Times. By Lord ARTHUR HERVEY, M.A. 8vo. 10s. 6d.

HERVEY (ROSAMOND). *Works by* ROSAMOND HERVEY.

The Aarbergs.
Two vols. crown 8vo. cloth. 21s.

Duke Ernest,
A Tragedy; and other Poems. Fcap. 8vo. 6s.

HILL (FLORENCE.)—*Children of the State. The Training of Juvenile Paupers.*
Extra fcap. cloth. 5s.

Historical Selections.
A Series of Readings from the best Authorities on English and European History. Selected and Arranged by E. M. SEWELL and C. M. YONGE. Extra fcap. 8vo. 6s.

HISTORICUS.—*Letters on some Questions of International Law.*
Reprinted from the *Times*, with considerable Additions. 8vo. 7s. 6d. Also, ADDITIONAL LETTERS. 8vo. 2s. 6d.

HODGSON.—*Mythology for Latin Versification.*
A Brief Sketch of the Fables of the Ancients, prepared to be rendered into Latin Verse for Schools. By F. HODGSON, B.D. late Provost of Eton. *New Edition,* revised by F. C. HODGSON, M.A. 18mo. 3s.

HOLE.—*Works by* CHARLES HOLE, M.A. *Trinity College, Cambridge.*

A Brief Biographical Dictionary.
Compiled and arranged by CHARLES HOLE, M.A. Trinity College, Cambridge. In pott 8vo. neatly and strongly bound in cloth. *Second Edition.* 4s. 6d.

Genealogical Stemma of the Kings of England and France.
In One Sheet. 1s.

HORNER.—*The Tuscan Poet Guiseppe Givsti and his Times.*
  By SUSAN HORNER. Crown 8vo. 7s. 6d.

HOWARD.—*The Pentateuch;*
  Or, the Five Books of Moses. Translated into English from the Version of the LXX. With Notes on its Omissions and Insertions, and also on the Passages in which it differs from the Authorized Version. By the Hon. HENRY HOWARD, D.D. Crown 8vo. GENESIS, One Volume, 8s. 6d.; EXODUS AND LEVITICUS, One Volume, 10s. 6d.; NUMBERS AND DEUTERONOMY, One Volume, 10s. 6d.

HOZIER.—*The Seven Weeks' War;*
  Its Antecedents and its Incidents. By H. M. HOZIER. With Maps and Plans. Two Vols. 8vo. 28s.

HUMPHRY.—*The Human Skeleton (including the Joints).*
  By G. M. HUMPHRY, M.D., F.R.S. With Two Hundred and Sixty Illustrations drawn from Nature. Medium 8vo. 1l. 8s.

HUXLEY.—*Lessons in Elementary Physiology.*
  With numerous Illustrations. By T. H. HUXLEY, F.R.S. Professor of Natural History in the Royal School of Mines. Uniform with Macmillans' School Class Books. *Second Edition.* 18mo. 4s. 6d.

Hymni Ecclesiæ.
  Fcap. 8vo. 7s. 6d.

IRVING.—*Annals of our Own Time.*
  A Diurnal of Events, Social and Political, which have happened in or had relation to the Kingdom of Great Britain from the Accession of Queen Victoria to the present Year. By JOSEPH IRVING. 8vo. [In the Press.

JAMESON.—*Works by the Rev. F. J. JAMESON, M.A.*
  Life's Work, in Preparation and in Retrospect.
    Sermons preached before the University of Cambridge. Fcap. 8vo. 1s. 6d.
  Brotherly Counsels to Students.
    Sermons preached in the Chapel of St. Catharine's College, Cambridge. Fcap. 8vo. 1s. 6d.

JEVONS.—*The Coal Question.*
  By W. STANLEY JEVONS, M.A. Fellow of University College, London. *Second Edition, revised.* 8vo. 10s. 6d.

JONES.—*The Church of England and Common Sense.*
  By HARRY JONES, M.A. Fcap. 8vo. 3s. 6d.

JONES.—*Algebraical Exercises,*
  Progressively Arranged by the Rev. C. A. JONES, M.A. and C. H. CHEYNE, M.A. Mathematical Masters in Westminster School. 18mo. 2s. 6d.

LIST OF PUBLICATIONS.

Journal of Anatomy and Physiology.
> Conducted by Professors HUMPHRY and NEWTON, and Mr. CLARK of Cambridge; Professor TURNER, of Edinburgh; and Dr. WRIGHT, of Dublin. Published twice a year. Price to subscribers, 14s. per annum. Price 7s. 6d. each Part. Vol. 1. containing Parts I. and II. Royal 8vo. 16s. Part III. 6s.

JUVENAL, *for Schools.*
> With English Notes. By J. E. B. MAYOR, M.A. *New and Cheaper Edition.* Crown 8vo. [In the Press.

KEARY.—*The Little Wanderlin,*
> And other Fairy Tales. By A. and E. KEARY. 16mo. 3s. 6d.

KEMPIS (THOS. A).—*De Imitatione Christi. Libri IV.*
> Borders in the ancient style, after Holbein, Durer, and other old Masters, containing Dances of Death, Acts of Mercy, Emblems, and a variety of curious ornamentation. In white cloth, extra gilt. 7s. 6d.

KENNEDY.—*Legendary Fictions of the Irish Celts.*
> Collected and Narrated by PATRICK KENNEDY. Crown 8vo. 7s. 6d.

KINGSBURY.—*Spiritual Sacrifice and Holy Communion.*
> Seven Sermons preached during the Lent of 1867 at St. Leonard's-on-Sea, with Notes. By T. L. KINGSBURY, M.A. late Rector of Chetwynd. Fcap. 8vo. 3s. 6d.

KINGSLEY.— *Works by the Rev.* CHARLES KINGSLEY, M.A. *Rector of Eversley, and Professor of Modern History in the University of Cambridge.*

> *The Roman and the Teuton.*
>> A Series of Lectures delivered before the University of Cambridge. 8vo. 12s.

> *Two Years Ago.*
>> *Fourth Edition.* Crown 8vo. 6s.

> "*Westward Ho!*"
>> *Fifth Edition.* Crown 8vo. 6s.

> *Alton Locke.*
>> *New Edition.* With a New Preface. Crown 8vo. 4s. 6d.

> *Hypatia.*
>> *Fourth Edition.* Crown 8vo. 6s.

> *Yeast.*
>> *Fifth Edition.* Crown 8vo. 5s.

> *Hereward the Wake—Last of the English.*
>> Crown 8vo. 6s.

KINGSLEY (*Rev.* CHARLES).—*The Saint's Tragedy.*
>Third Edition. Fcap. 8vo. 5s.

Andromeda,
>And other Poems. Third Edition. Fcap. 8vo. 5s.

The Water Babies.
>A Fairy Tale for a Land Baby. With Two Illustrations by Sir NOEL PATON, R.S.A. Third Edition. Crown 8vo. 6s.

The Heroes;
>Or, Greek Fairy Tales for my Children. With Coloured Illustrations. New Edition. 18mo. 4s. 6d.

Three Lectures delivered at the Royal Institution on the Ancien Régime.
>Crown 8vo. 6s.

The Water of Life,
>And other Sermons. Fcap. 8vo. 6s.

Village Sermons.
>Seventh Edition. Fcap. 8vo. 2s. 6d.

The Gospel of the Pentateuch.
>Second Edition. Fcap. 8vo. 4s. 6d.

Good News of God.
>Fourth Edition. Fcap. 8vo. 4s. 6d.

Sermons for the Times.
>Third Edition. Fcap. 8vo. 3s. 6d.

Town and Country Sermons.
>Extra fcap. 8vo. New Edition. 6s.

Sermons on National Subjects.
>First Series. Second Edition. Fcap. 8vo. 5s.
>Second Series. Second Edition. Fcap. 8vo. 5s.

Discipline,
>And other Sermons. Fcap. 8vo. 6s.

Alexandria and her Schools.
>With a Preface. Crown 8vo. 5s.

The Limits of Exact Science as applied to History.
>An Inaugural Lecture delivered before the University of Cambridge. Crown 8vo. 2s.

Phaethon; or, Loose Thoughts for Loose Thinkers.
>Third Edition. Crown 8vo. 2s.

David.
>Four Sermons: David's Weakness—David's Strength—David's Anger—David's Deserts. Fcap. 8vo. cloth. 2s. 6d.

KINGSLEY.—*Works by* HENRY KINGSLEY.
   Austin Elliot.
      New Edition. Crown 8vo. 6s.
   The Recollections of Geoffry Hamlyn.
      Second Edition. Crown 8vo. 6s.
   The Hillyars and the Burtons: A Story of Two Families.
      Crown 8vo. 6s.
   Ravenshoe.
      New Edition. Crown 8vo. 6s.
   Leighton Court.
      New Edition. Crown 8vo. 6s.
   Silcote of Silcotes.
      Three Vols. Crown 8vo. 31s. 6d.

KIRCHHOFF.—*Researches on the Solar Spectrum and the Spectra of the Chemical Elements.*
      By G. KIRCHHOFF, of Heidelberg. Translated by HENRY E. ROSCOE, B.A. Second Part. 4to. 5s. with 2 Plates.

KITCHENER.—*Geometrical Note Book,*
      Containing Easy Problems in Geometrical Drawing, preparatory to the Study of Geometry. For the Use of Schools. By F. E. KITCHENER, M.A., Mathematical Master at Rugby. 4to. 2s.

LANCASTER.—*Works by* WILLIAM LANCASTER.
   Præterita.
      Poems. Extra fcap. 8vo. 4s. 6d.
   Studies in Verse.
      Extra fcap. 8vo. 4s. 6d.
   Eclogues and Mono-dramas; or, a Collection of Verses.
      Extra fcap. 8vo. 4s. 6d.

LATHAM.—*The Construction of Wrought-iron Bridges.*
      Embracing the Practical Application of the Principles of Mechanics to Wrought-Iron Girder Work. By J. H. LATHAM, Civil Engineer. 8vo. With numerous detail Plates. *Second Edition.* [Preparing.

LATHAM.—*Black and White: A Three Months' Tour in the United States.*
      By H. LATHAM, M.A. Barrister-at-Law. 8vo. 10s. 6d.

LAW.—*The Alps of Hannibal.*
      By WILLIAM JOHN LAW, M.A. Two vols. 8vo. 21s.

Lectures to Ladies on Practical Subjects.
    Third Edition, revised. Crown 8vo. 7s. 6d.

LEMON.—*Legends of Number Nip.*
    By MARK LEMON. With Six Illustrations by CHARLES KEENE. Extra fcap. 8vo. 5s.

LIGHTFOOT.—*Works by J. B. LIGHTFOOT, D.D. Hulsean Professor of Divinity in the University of Cambridge.*

St. Paul's Epistle to the Galatians.
    A Revised Text, with Notes and Dissertations. Second Edition, revised. 8vo. 12s.

St. Paul's Epistle to the Philippians.
    A Revised Text, with Notes and Dissertations. 8vo. 12s.

Little Estella.
    And other Fairy Tales for the Young. Royal 16mo. 3s. 6d.

LIVERPOOL.—*The Life and Administration of Robert Banks, Second Earl of Liverpool.*
    Compiled from Original Documents by PROFESSOR YONGE. 3 vols. 8vo. 42s.

LOCKYER.—*Elementary Lessons in Astronomy. With numerous Illustrations.*
    By J. NORMAN LOCKYER, F.R.A.S. 18mo. 5s. 6d.

LUCKOCK.—*The Tables of Stone.*
    A Course of Sermons preached in All Saints', Cambridge, by H. M. LUCKOCK, M.A., Vicar. Fcap. 8vo. 3s. 6d.

LUDLOW and HUGHES.—*A Sketch of the History of the United States from Independence to Secession.*
    By J. M. LUDLOW, Author of "British India, its Races and its History," "The Policy of the Crown towards India," &c. To which is added, "The Struggle for Kansas." By THOMAS HUGHES, Author of "Tom Brown's School Days," "Tom Brown at Oxford," &c. Crown 8vo. 8s. 6d.

LUSHINGTON.—*The Italian War, 1848-9, and the Last Italian Poet.*
    By the late HENRY LUSHINGTON. With a Biographical Preface by G. S. VENABLES. Crown 8vo. 6s. 6d.

LYTTELTON.—*Works by LORD LYTTELTON.*

The Comus of Milton rendered into Greek Verse.
    Extra fcap. 8vo. Second Edition. 5s.

The Samson Agonistes of Milton rendered into Greek Verse.
    Extra fcap. 8vo. 6s. 6d.

MACKENZIE.—*The Christian Clergy of the First Ten Centuries, and their Influence on European Civilization.*
 By HENRY MACKENZIE, B.A. Scholar of Trinity College, Cambridge. Crown 8vo. 6s. 6d.

MACLAREN.—*Sermons preached at Manchester.*
 By ALEXANDER MACLAREN. Second Edition. Fcap. 8vo. 4s. 6d. A Second Series in the Press.

MACLAREN.—*Training, in Theory and Practice.*
 By ARCHIBALD MACLAREN, Oxford. With Frontispiece, and other Illustrations. 8vo. Handsomely bound in cloth. 7s. 6d.

MACLEAR.— *Works by* G. F. MACLEAR, B.D. *Head Master of King's College School, and Preacher at the Temple Church :*—

 A History of Christian Missions during the Middle Ages.
  Crown 8vo. 10s. 6d.

 The Witness of the Eucharist; or, The Institution and Early Celebration of the Lord's Supper, considered as an Evidence of the Historical Truth of the Gospel Narrative and of the Atonement.
  Crown 8vo. 4s. 6d.

 A Class-Book of Old Testament History.
  With Four Maps. Fourth Edition. 18mo. 4s. 6d.

 A Class-Book of New Testament History.
  Including the connexion of the Old and New Testament. Second Edition. 18mo. 5s. 6d.

 A Class-Book of the Catechism of the Church of England.
  Second Edition. 18mo. cloth. 2s. 6d.

 A Shilling Book of Old Testament History.
  18mo. cloth limp. 1s.

 A Shilling Book of New Testament History.
  18mo. cloth limp. 1s.

 A First Class-Book of the Catechism of the Church of England, with Scripture Proofs for Junior Classes and Schools.
  6d.

MACMILLAN.—*Works by the Rev.* HUGH MACMILLAN.
   Bible Teachings in Nature.
      Second Edition. Crown 8vo. 6s.

   Foot-notes from the Page of Nature.
      With numerous Illustrations. Fcap. 8vo. 5s.

Macmillan's Magazine.
      Published Monthly, price One Shilling. Volumes I.—XVIII. are now ready, 7s. 6d. each.

MACMILLAN & CO.'S *Six Shilling Series of Works of Fiction.*

KINGSLEY.—*Works by the* REV. CHARLES KINGSLEY, M.A.
   Westward Ho!
   Hypatia.
   Hereward the Wake—Last of the English.
   Two Years Ago.

Works by the Author of "The Heir of Redclyffe."
   The Heir of Redclyffe.
   Dynevor Terrace; or, The Clue of Life.
   Heartsease; or, The Brother's Wife.
   The Clever Woman of the Family.
   Hopes and Fears; or, Scenes from the Life of a Spinster
   The Young Stepmother; or, A Chronicle of Mistakes.
   The Daisy Chain.
   The Trial: More Links of the Daisy Chain.

KINGSLEY.—*Works by* HENRY KINGSLEY.
   Geoffry Hamlyn.
   Ravenshoe.
   Austin Elliot.
   Hillyars and Burtons.
   Leighton Court.

TREVELYAN.—*Works by* G. O. TREVELYAN.
  Cawnpore.
  Competition Wallah.

MISCELLANEOUS.
  The Moor Cottage.
    By MAY BEVERLEY.
  Janet's Home.
  Tom Brown at Oxford.
    By the Author of "Tom Brown's School Days."
  Clemency Franklyn.
    By the Author of "Janet's Home."
  A Son of the Soil.
  Old Sir Douglas.
    By HON. MRS. NORTON.

McCOSH.—*Works by* JAMES McCOSH, LL.D. *Professor of Logic and Metaphysics, Queen's College, Belfast, &c.*
  The Method of the Divine Government, Physical and Moral.
    Ninth Edition. 8vo. 10s. 6d.
  The Supernatural in Relation to the Natural.
    Crown 8vo. 7s. 6d.
  The Intuitions of the Mind.
    A New Edition. 8vo. 10s. 6d.
  An Examination of Mr. J. S. Mill's Philosophy.
    Being a Defence of Fundamental Truth. Crown 8vo. 7s. 6d.
  Philosophical Papers.
    I. Examination of Sir W. Hamilton's Logic. II. Reply to Mr. Mill's Third Edition. III. Present State of Moral Philosophy in Britain. 8vo. 3s. 6d.

MANSFIELD.—*Works by* C. B. MANSFIELD, M.A.
  Paraguay, Brazil, and the Plate.
    With a Map, and numerous Woodcuts. With a Sketch of his Life, by the Rev. CHARLES KINGSLEY. Crown 8vo. 12s. 6d.
  A Theory of Salts.
    A Treatise on the Constitution of Bipolar (two membered) Chemical Compounds. Crown 8vo. cloth. 14s.

MARKHAM.—*A History of the Abyssinian Expedition.*
> Including an Account of the Physical Geography, Geology, and Botany of the Region traversed by the English Forces. By CLEMENTS R. MARKHAM, F.R.G.S. With a Chapter by LIEUT. PRIDEAUX, containing a Narrative of his Mission and Captivity. With Maps, &c. 8vo.

MARRINER.—*Sermons preached at Lyme Regis.*
> By E. T. MARRINER, Curate. Fcap. 8vo. 4s. 6d.

MARSHALL.—*A Table of Irregular Greek Verbs.*
> 8vo. 1s.

MARTIN.—*The Statesman's Year Book for 1869.* By FREDERICK MARTIN. (*Sixth Annual Publication.*)
> A Statistical, Mercantile, and Historical Account of the Civilized World for the Year 1868. Forming a Manual for Politicians and Merchants. Crown 8vo. 10s. 6d.

MARTINEAU.—*Biographical Sketches, 1852–68.*
> By HARRIET MARTINEAU.

MASSON.—*Works by* DAVID MASSON, M.A. *Professor of Rhetoric and English Literature in the University of Edinburgh.*

> *Essays, Biographical and Critical.*
>> Chiefly on the English Poets. 8vo. 12s. 6d.

> *British Novelists and their Styles.*
>> Being a Critical Sketch of the History of British Prose Fiction. Crown 8vo. 7s. 6d.

> *Life of John Milton.*
>> Narrated in connexion with the Political, Ecclesiastical, and Literary History of his Time. Vol. I. with Portraits. 8vo. 18s.

> *Recent British Philosophy.*
>> A Review, with Criticisms, including some Comments on Mr. Mill's Answer to Sir William Hamilton. *New and Cheaper Edition.* Crown 8vo. 6s.

MAUDSLEY.—*The Physiology and Pathology of the Mind.*
> By HENRY MAUDSLEY, M.D. *New and Revised Edition.* 8vo. 16s.

MAURICE.—*Works by the Rev.* FREDERICK DENISON MAURICE, M.A. *Professor of Moral Philosophy in the University of Cambridge.*

> *The Conscience.*
>> Lectures on Casuistry, delivered in the University of Cambridge. 8vo. 8s. 6d.

LIST OF PUBLICATIONS.

MAURICE.—*The Claims of the Bible and of Science.*
A Correspondence on some Questions respecting the Pentateuch.
Crown 8vo. 4s. 6d.

Dialogues on Family Worship.
Crown 8vo. 6s.

The Patriarchs and Lawgivers of the Old Testament.
Third and Cheaper Edition. Crown 8vo. 5s.
This volume contains Discourses on the Pentateuch, Joshua, Judges, and the beginning of the First Book of Samuel.

The Prophets and Kings of the Old Testament.
Second Edition. Crown 8vo. 10s. 6d.
This volume contains Discourses on Samuel I. and II.; Kings I. and II.; Amos, Joel, Hosea, Isaiah, Micah, Nahum, Habakkuk, Jeremiah, and Ezekiel.

The Gospel of the Kingdom of Heaven.
A Series of Lectures on the Gospel of St. Luke. Crown 8vo. 9s.

The Gospel of St. John.
A Series of Discourses. Third and Cheaper Edition. Crown 8vo. 6s.

The Epistles of St. John.
A Series of Lectures on Christian Ethics. Second and Cheaper Edition. Crown 8vo. 6s.

The Commandments considered as Instruments of National Reformation.
Crown 8vo. 4s. 6d.

Expository Sermons on the Prayer-book. The Prayer-book considered especially in reference to the Romish System.
Second Edition. Fcap. 8vo. 5s. 6d.

Lectures on the Apocalypse,
Or Book of the Revelation of St. John the Divine. Crown 8vo. 10s. 6d.

What is Revelation?
A Series of Sermons on the Epiphany; to which are added Letters to a Theological Student on the Bampton Lectures of Mr. MANSEL. Crown 8vo. 10s. 6d.

Sequel to the Inquiry, "What is Revelation?"
Letters in Reply to Mr. Mansel's Examination of "Strictures on the Bampton Lectures." Crown 8vo. 6s.

Lectures on Ecclesiastical History.
8vo. 10s. 6d.

MAURICE.—*Theological Essays.*
    Second Edition. Crown 8vo. 10s. 6d.
The Doctrine of Sacrifice deduced from the Scriptures.
    Crown 8vo. 7s. 6d.
The Religions of the World,
    And their Relations to Christianity. *Fourth Edition.* Fcap. 8vo. 5s.
On the Lord's Prayer.
    Fourth Edition. Fcap. 8vo. 2s. 6d.
On the Sabbath Day;
    The Character of the Warrior; and on the Interpretation of History. Fcap. 8vo. 2s. 6d.
Learning and Working.
    Six Lectures on the Foundation of Colleges for Working Men. Crown 8vo. 5s.
The Ground and Object of Hope for Mankind.
    Four Sermons preached before the University of Cambridge. Crown 8vo. 3s. 6d.
Law's Remarks on the Fable of the Bees.
    With an Introduction by F. D. MAURICE, M.A. Fcap. 8vo. 4s. 6d.

MAYOR.—*A First Greek Reader.*
    Edited after Karl Halm, with Corrections and Additions. By JOHN E. B. MAYOR, M.A. Fcap. 8vo. 6s.
Autobiography of Matthew Robinson.
    By JOHN E. B. MAYOR, M.A. Fcap. 8vo. 5s. 6d.

MERIVALE.—*Sallust for Schools.*
    By C. MERIVALE, B.D. Second Edition. Fcap. 8vo. 4s. 6d.
    ₊ The Jugurtha and the Catalina may be had separately, price 2s. 6d. each.
Keats' Hyperion rendered into Latin Verse.
    By C. MERIVALE, B.D. Second Edition. Extra fcap. 8vo. 3s. 6d.

MISTRAL, F.—*Mirelle, a Pastoral Epic of Provence.*
    Translated by H. CRICHTON. Extra fcap. 8vo. 6s.

Modern Industries: A Series of Reports on Industry and Manufactures as represented in the Paris Exposition in 1867.
    By TWELVE BRITISH WORKMEN. Crown 8vo. 1s.

MOORHOUSE.—*Works by* JAMES MOORHOUSE, M.A.
  Some Modern Difficulties respecting the Facts of Nature and Revelation.
    Fcap. 8vo. 2s. 6d.

  The Hulsean Lectures for 1865.
    Crown 8vo. 5s.

MORGAN.—*A Collection of Mathematical Problems and Examples.*
    By H. A. MORGAN, M.A. Crown 8vo. 6s. 6d.

MORISON.—*The Life and Times of Saint Bernard, Abbot of Clairvaux.*
    By JAMES COTTER MORISON, M.A. *New Edition, revised.* Crown 8vo. 7s. 6d.

MORLEY, JOHN.—*Edmund Burke—a Historical Study.*
    Crown 8vo. 7s. 6d.

MORSE.—*Working for God,*
  And other Practical Sermons. By FRANCIS MORSE, M.A. *Second Edition.* Fcap. 8vo. 5s.

MULLINGER.—*Cambridge Characteristics in the Seventeenth Century.*
    By J. B. MULLINGER, B.A. Crown 8vo. 4s. 6d.

MYERS.—*St. Paul.*
    A Poem. By F. W. H. MYERS. *Second Edition.* Extra fcap. 8vo. 2s. 6d.

NETTLESHIP.—*Essays on Robert Browning's Poetry.*
    By JOHN T. NETTLESHIP. Extra fcap. 8vo. 6s. 6d.

New Landlord, The.
    Translated from the Hungarian of MAURICE JOKAI by A. J. PATTERSON. Two vols. crown 8vo. 21s.

Northern Circuit.
    Brief Notes of Travel in Sweden, Finland, and Russia. With a Frontispiece. Crown 8vo. 5s.

NORTON.—*The Lady of La Garaye.*
    By the Hon. Mrs. NORTON. With Vignette and Frontispiece. *Sixth Edition.* Fcap. 8vo. 4s. 6d.

O'BRIEN.—*Works by* JAMES THOMAS O'BRIEN, D.D. *Bishop of Ossory.*

An Attempt to Explain and Establish the Doctrine of Justification by Faith only.
Third Edition. 8vo. 12s.

Charge delivered at the Visitation in 1863.
Second Edition. 8vo. 2s.

OLIPHANT.—*Agnes Hopetoun's Schools and Holidays.*
By Mrs. OLIPHANT. Royal 16mo. gilt leaves. 3s. 6d.

OLIVER.—*Lessons in Elementary Botany.*
With nearly 200 Illustrations. By DANIEL OLIVER, F.R.S. F.L.S. 18mo. 4s. 6d.

OPPEN.—*French Reader,*
For the Use of Colleges and Schools. By EDWARD A. OPPEN. Fcap. 8vo. 4s. 6d.

ORWELL.—*The Bishop's Walk and the Bishop's Times.*
Poems on the Days of Archbishop Leighton and the Scottish Covenant. By ORWELL. Fcap. 8vo. 5s.

Our Year.
A Child's Book, in Prose and Verse. By the Author of "John Halifax, Gentleman." Illustrated by CLARENCE DOBELL. Royal 16mo. 3s. 6d.

PALGRAVE.—*History of Normandy and of England.*
By Sir FRANCIS PALGRAVE. Completing the History to the Death of William Rufus. Vols. I. to IV. 8vo. each 21s.

PALGRAVE.—*A Narrative of a Year's Journey through Central and Eastern Arabia,* 1862-3.
By WILLIAM GIFFORD PALGRAVE (late of the Eighth Regiment Bombay N.I.) *Fourth and Cheaper Edition.* With Map, Plans and Portrait of Author, engraved on Steel by JEENS. Crown 8vo. 7s. 6d.

PALGRAVE.—*Works by* FRANCIS TURNER PALGRAVE, M.A. *late Fellow of Exeter College, Oxford.*

The Five Days' Entertainments at Wentworth Grange.
Small 4to. 9s.

PALGRAVE.—*Essays on Art.*
Mulready—Dyce—Holman Hunt—Herbert—Poetry, Prose, and Sensationalism in Art—Sculpture in England—The Albert Cross, &c. Extra fcap. 8vo. 6s.

Sonnets and Songs.
By WILLIAM SHAKESPEARE. GEM EDITION. With Vignette Title by JEENS. 3s. 6d.

Original Hymns.
Second Edition, enlarged. 18mo. 1s. 6d.

PALMER.—*The Book of Praise:*
From the Best English Hymn Writers. Selected and arranged by SIR ROUNDELL PALMER. With Vignette by WOOLNER. 18mo. 4s. 6d. *Large Type Edition*, demy 8vo. 10s. 6d. morocco, 21s.

A Hymnal.
Chiefly from the BOOK OF PRAISE. In various sizes.
A.—In royal 32mo. cloth limp. 6d.
B.—Small 18mo. larger type, cloth limp. 1s.
C.—Same Edition, fine paper, cloth. 1s. 6d.

An Edition with Music, Selected, Harmonized, and Composed by JOHN HULLAH. Square 18mo. 3s. 6d.

PARKINSON.—*Works by* S. PARKINSON, B.D.

A Treatise on Elementary Mechanics.
For the Use of the Junior Classes at the University and the Higher Classes in Schools. With a Collection of Examples. *Third Edition, revised.* Crown 8vo. 9s. 6d.

A Treatise on Optics.
Second Edition, revised. Crown 8vo. 10s. 6d.

PATMORE.—*Works by* COVENTRY PATMORE.

The Angel in the House.
Book I. The Betrothal.—Book II. The Espousals.—Book III. Faithful for Ever. With Tamerton Church Tower. Two vols. fcap. 8vo. 12s.
*** A New and Cheap Edition, in one vol. 18mo. beautifully printed on toned paper, price 2s. 6d.

The Victories of Love.
Fcap. 8vo. 4s. 6d.

Phantasmagoria and other Poems.
By LEWIS CARROLL.

PHEAR.—*Elementary Hydrostatics.*
By J. B. PHEAR, M.A. *Third Edition.* Crown 8vo. 5s. 6d.

PHILLIMORE.—*Private Law among the Romans.*
 From the Pandects. By JOHN GEORGE PHILLIMORE, Q.C. 8vo. 16s.

Philology.
 The Journal of Sacred and Classical Philology. Four Vols. 8vo. 12s. 6d. each.

 The Journal of Philology. New Series. Edited by W. G. CLARK, M.A. JOHN E. B. MAYOR, M.A. and W. ALDIS WRIGHT, M.A. No. I. 8vo. 4s. 6d. (Half-yearly.)

PLATO.—*The Republic of Plato.*
 Translated into English, with Notes. By Two Fellows of Trinity College, Cambridge (J. LL Davies, M.A. and D. J. Vaughan, M.A.). With Vignette Portraits of Plato and Socrates engraved by JEENS from an Antique Gem. (Golden Treasury Series.) *New Edition*, 18mo. 4s. 6d.

Platonic Dialogues, The,
 For English Readers. By the late W. WHEWELL, D.D. F.R.S. Master of Trinity College, Cambridge. Vol. I. *Second Edition*, containing *The Socratic Dialogues*, fcap. 8vo. 7s. 6d.; Vol. II. containing *The Anti-Sophist Dialogues*, 6s. 6d.; Vol. III. containing *The Republic*, 7s. 6d.

Plea for a New English Version of the Scriptures.
 By a Licentiate of the Church of Scotland. 8vo. 6s.

POTTER.—*A Voice from the Church in Australia :*
 Sermons preached in Melbourne. By the Rev. ROBERT POTTER, M.A. Extra fcap. 8vo. 4s. 6d.

Practitioner (The), a Monthly Journal of Therapeutics.
 Edited by FRANCIS E. ANSTIE, M.D. and HENRY LAWSON, M.D. 8vo. Price 1s. 6d.

PRATT.—*Treatise on Attractions, La Place's Functions, and the Figure of the Earth.*
 By J. H. PRATT, M.A. *Third Edition*. Crown 8vo. 6s. 6d.

PRESCOTT.—*The Threefold Cord.*
 Sermons preached before the University of Cambridge. By J. E. PRESCOTT, B.D. Fcap. 8vo. 3s. 6d.

PROCTER.—*Works by* FRANCIS PROCTER, M.A.

 A History of the Book of Common Prayer :
  With a Rationale of its Offices. *Seventh Edition, revised and enlarged*. Crown 8vo. 10s. 6d.

PROCTER AND G. F. MACLEAR, B.D.—*An Elementary History of the Book of Common Prayer. New Edition.*
 18mo. 2s. 6d.

Psalms of David chronologically arranged.
An Amended Version, with Historical Introductions and Explanatory Notes. By FOUR FRIENDS. Crown 8vo. 10s. 6d.

PUCKLE.—*An Elementary Treatise on Conic Sections and Algebraic Geometry, with numerous Examples and Hints for their Solution,*
Especially designed for the Use of Beginners. By G. HALE PUCKLE, M.A. Head Master of Windermere College. *Third Edition, enlarged.* Crown 8vo. 7s. 6d.

PULLEN.—*The Psalter and Canticles, Pointed for Chanting,*
With Marks of Expression, and a List of Appropriate Chants. By the Rev. HENRY PULLEN, M.A. 8vo. 5s.

RALEGH.—*The Life of Sir Walter Ralegh, based upon Contemporary Documents.*
By EDWARD EDWARDS. Together with his LETTERS, now first Collected. With Portrait. Two Vols. 8vo. 32s.

RAMSAY.—*The Catechiser's Manual ;*
Or, the Church Catechism Illustrated and Explained, for the Use of Clergymen, Schoolmasters, and Teachers. By ARTHUR RAMSAY, M.A. *Second Edition.* 18mo. 1s. 6d.

RAWLINSON.—*Elementary Statics.*
By G. RAWLINSON, M.A. Edited by EDWARD STURGES, M.A. Crown 8vo. 4s. 6d.

Rays of Sunlight for Dark Days.
A Book of Selections for the Suffering. With a Preface by C. J. VAUGHAN, D.D. 18mo. *New Edition.* 3s. 6d. Morocco, old style, 7s. 6d.

Reform.—Essays on Reform.
By the Hon. G. C. BRODRICK, R. H. HUTTON, LORD HOUGHTON, A. V. DICEY, LESLIE STEPHEN, J. B. KINNEAR, B. CRACROFT, C. H. PEARSON, GOLDWIN SMITH, JAMES BRYCE, A. L. RUTSON, and Sir GEO. YOUNG. 8vo. 10s. 6d.

Questions for a Reformed Parliament.
By F. H. HILL, GODFREY LUSHINGTON, MEREDITH TOWNSEND, W. L. NEWMAN, C. S. PARKER, J. B. KINNEAR, G. HOOPER, F. HARRISON, Rev. J. E. T. ROGERS, J. M. LUDLOW, and LLOYD JONES. 8vo. 10s. 6d.

REYNOLDS.—*A System of Medicine.* Vol. I.
  Edited by J. RUSSELL REYNOLDS, M.D. F.R.C.P. London. PART I. GENERAL DISEASES, or Affections of the Whole System. § I.—Those determined by agents operating from without, such as the exanthemata, malarial diseases, and their allies. § II.—Those determined by conditions existing within the body, such as Gout, Rheumatism, Rickets, &c. PART II. LOCAL DISEASES, or Affections of particular Systems. § I.— Diseases of the Skin. 8vo. 25s.

REYNOLDS.—*A System of Medicine.* Vol. II.
  PART II. § I.—Diseases of the Nervous System. A. General Nervous Diseases. B. Partial Diseases of the Nervous System. 1. Diseases of the Head. 2. Diseases of the Spinal Column. 3. Diseases of the Nerves. § II.—Diseases of the Digestive System. A. Diseases of the Stomach. 8vo. 25s.

  Notes of the Christian Life.
    A Selection of Sermons by HENRY ROBERT REYNOLDS, B.A. President of Cheshunt College, and Fellow of University College, London. Crown 8vo. 7s. 6d.

REYNOLDS.—*Modern Methods of Elementary Geometry.*
  By E. M. REYNOLDS, M.A. Mathematical Master in Clifton College. Crown 8vo. 3s. 6d.

Ridicula Rediviva.
  Being old Nursery Rhymes. With Coloured Illustrations by J. E. ROGERS. 9s.

ROBERTS.—*Discussions on the Gospels.*
  By the Rev. ALEXANDER ROBERTS, D.D. *Second Edition, revised and enlarged.* 8vo. 16s.

ROBERTSON.—*Pastoral Counsels.*
  By the late JOHN ROBERTSON, D.D. of Glasgow Cathedral. New Edition. With Biographical Sketch by the Author of "Recreations of a Country Parson." Extra fcap. 8vo. 6s.

ROBINSON CRABB.—*Life and Reminiscences.* [In the Press.

ROBY.—*A Latin Grammar for the Higher Classes in Grammar Schools, based on the "Elementary Latin Grammar."*
  By H. J. ROBY, M.A. [In the Press.

ROBY.—*Story of a Household, and other Poems.*
  By MARY K. ROBY. Fcap. 8vo. 5s.

ROMANIS.—*Sermons preached at St. Mary's, Reading.*
  By WILLIAM ROMANIS, M.A. *First Series.* Fcap. 8vo 6s Also, *Second Series.* 6s.

LIST OF PUBLICATIONS.

ROSCOE.—*Lessons in Elementary Chemistry, Inorganic and Organic.*
  By H. E. ROSCOE, F.R.S. *Eighth Thousand.* 18mo. 4s. 6d.

ROSSETTI.—*Works by* CHRISTINA ROSSETTI.
  Goblin Market, and other Poems.
    With Two Designs by D. G. ROSSETTI. *Second Edition.* Fcap. 8vo. 5s.
  The Prince's Progress, and other Poems.
    With Two Designs by D. G. ROSSETTI. Fcap. 8vo. 6s.

ROSSETTI.—*Works by* WILLIAM MICHAEL ROSSETTI.
  Dante's Comedy, The Hell.
    Translated into Literal Blank Verse. Fcap. 8vo. 5s.
  Fine Art, chiefly Contemporary.
    Crown 8vo. 10s. 6d.

ROUTH.—*Treatise on Dynamics of Rigid Bodies.*
  With Numerous Examples. By E. J. ROUTH, M.A. *New Edition.* Crown 8vo. 14s.

ROWSELL.—*Works by* T. J. ROWSELL, M.A.
  The English Universities and the English Poor.
    Sermons preached before the University of Cambridge. Fcap. 8vo. 2s.
  Man's Labour and God's Harvest.
    Sermons preached before the University of Cambridge in Lent, 1861. Fcap. 8vo. 3s.

RUFFINI.—*Vincenzo ; or, Sunken Rocks.*
  By JOHN RUFFINI. Three vols. crown 8vo. 31s. 6d.

Ruth and her Friends.
  A Story for Girls. With a Frontispiece. *Fourth Edition.* Royal 16mo. 3s. 6d.

SCOTT.—*Discourses.*
  By A. J. SCOTT, M.A. late Professor of Logic in Owens College, Manchester. Crown 8vo. 7s. 6d.

Scouring of the White Horse.
  Or, the Long Vacation Ramble of a London Clerk. By the Author of "Tom Brown's School Days." Illustrated by DOYLE. *Eighth Thousand.* Imp. 16mo. 8s. 6d.

SEATON.—*A Hand-Book of Vaccination.*
  By EDWARD C. SEATON, M.D. Medical Inspector to the Privy Council. Extra fcap. 8vo. 8s. 6d.

SELKIRK.—*Guide to the Cricket Ground.*
By G. H. SELKIRK. With Woodcuts. Extra Fcap. 8vo. 3s. 6d.

SELWYN.—*The Work of Christ in the World.*
By G. A. SELWYN, D.D. Bishop of Lichfield. Third Edition. Crown 8vo. 2s.

SHAKESPEARE.—*The Works of William Shakespeare.* Cambridge Edition.
Edited by WM. GEORGE CLARK, M.A. and W. ALDIS WRIGHT, M.A. Nine Vols. 8vo. cloth. 4l. 14s. 6d.

Shakespeare's Tempest.
With Glossarial and Explanatory Notes. By the Rev. J. M. JEPHSON. 18mo. 1s. 6d.

SHAIRP.—*Kilmahoe, and other Poems.*
By J. CAMPBELL SHAIRP. Fcap. 8vo. 5s.

SHIRLEY.—*Elijah; Four University Sermons.*
I. Samaria. II. Carmel. III. Kishon. IV. Horeb. By W. W. SHIRLEY, D.D. Fcap. 8vo. 2s. 6d.

SIMPSON.—*An Epitome of the History of the Christian Church.*
By WILLIAM SIMPSON, M.A. Fourth Edition. Fcap. 8vo. 3s. 6d.

SMITH.—*Works by* ALEXANDER SMITH.

A Life Drama, and other Poems.
Fcap. 8vo. 2s. 6d.

City Poems.
Fcap. 8vo. 5s.

Edwin of Deira.
Second Edition. Fcap. 8vo. 5s.

SMITH.—*Poems by* CATHERINE BARNARD SMITH.
Crown 8vo. 5s.

SMITH.—*Works by* GOLDWIN SMITH.

A Letter to a Whig Member of the Southern Independence Association.
Extra fcap. 8vo. 2s.

Three English Statesmen; Pym, Cromwell, and Pitt.
A Course of Lectures on the Political History of England. Extra fcap. 8vo. *New and Cheaper Edition.* 5s.

LIST OF PUBLICATIONS. 37

SMITH.— *Works by* BARNARD SMITH, M.A. *Rector of Glaston, Rutland, &c.*

Arithmetic and Algebra.
Tenth Edition. Crown 8vo. 10s. 6d.

Arithmetic for the Use of Schools.
Ninth Edition. Crown 8vo. 4s. 6d.

A Key to the Arithmetic for Schools.
Fifth Edition. Crown 8vo. 8s. 6d.

Exercises in Arithmetic.
With Answers. Cr. 8vo. limp cloth, 2s. 6d. Or sold separately as follows:—Part I. 1s. Part II. 1s. Answers, 6d.

School Class Book of Arithmetic.
18mo. 3s. Or sold separately, Parts I. and II. 10d. each. Part III. 1s.

Keys to School Class Book of Arithmetic.
Complete in One Volume, 18mo. 6s. 6d.; or Parts I. II. and III. 2s. 6d. each.

Shilling Book of Arithmetic for National and Elementary Schools.
18mo. cloth. Or separately, Part I. 2d.; II. 3d.; III. 7d.

Answers to the Shilling Book of Arithmetic.
18mo. 6d.

Key to the Shilling Book of Arithmetic.
18mo. 4s. 6d.

Examination Papers in Arithmetic.
In Four Parts. 18mo. 1s. 6d. With Answers, 1s. 9d.

Key to Examination Papers in Arithmetic.
18mo. 4s. 6d.

SMITH.—*Hymns of Christ and the Christian Life.*
By the Rev. WALTER C. SMITH, M.A. Fcap. 8vo. 6s.

SMITH.—*Obstacles to Missionary Success among the Heathen.*
The Maitland Prize Essay for 1867. By W. S. SMITH, M.A. Fellow of Trinity College, Cambridge. Crown 8vo. 3s. 6d.

SMITH.—*A Treatise on Elementary Statics.*
By J. H. SMITH, M.A. Gonville and Caius College, Cambridge Royal 8vo. 5s. 6d.

SMITH.—*A Treatise on Elementary Trigonometry.*
    Royal 8vo. 5s.

A Treatise on Elementary Hydrostatics.
    Royal 8vo. 4s. 6d.

SNOWBALL.—*The Elements of Plane and Spherical Trigonometry.*
    By J. C. SNOWBALL, M.A. Tenth Edition. Crown 8vo. 7s. 6d.

Social Duties considered with Reference to the Organization of Effort in Works of Benevolence and Public Utility.
    By a MAN OF BUSINESS. Fcap. 8vo. 4s. 6d.

SPENCER.—*Elements of Qualitative Chemical Analysis.*
    By W. H. SPENCER, B.A. 4to. 10s. 6d.

Spring Songs.
    By a WEST HIGHLANDER. With a Vignette Illustration by GOURLAY STEELE. Fcap. 8vo. 1s. 6d.

STEPHEN.—*General View of the Criminal Law of England.*
    By J. FITZ-JAMES STEPHEN. 8vo. 18s.

STRATFORD DE REDCLIFFE.—*Shadows of the Past, in Verse.*
    By VISCOUNT STRATFORD DE REDCLIFFE. Crown 8vo. 10s. 6d.

STRICKLAND.—*On Cottage Construction and Design.*
    By C. W. STRICKLAND. With Specifications and Plans. 8vo. 7s. 6d.

Sunday Library for Household Reading. Illustrated.
    Monthly Parts, 1s.; Quarterly Vols. 4s. Gilt edges, 4s. 6d.
    Vol. I.—The Pupils of St. John the Divine, by the Author of "The Heir of Redclyffe."
    Vol. II.—The Hermits, by PROFESSOR KINGSLEY.
    Vol. III.—Seekers after God, by the Rev. F. W. FARRAR.
    Vol. IV.—England's Antiphon, by GEORGE MACDONALD, LL.D.

SWAINSON.—*Works by* C. A. SWAINSON, D.D.

A Handbook to Butler's Analogy.
    Crown 8vo. 1s. 6d.

The Creeds of the Church in their Relations to Holy Scripture and the Conscience of the Christian.
    8vo. cloth. 9s.

The Authority of the New Testament,
    And other Lectures, delivered before the University of Cambridge. 8vo. cloth. 12s.

TACITUS.—*The History of Tacitus translated into English.*
By A. J. CHURCH, M.A. and W. J. BRODRIBB, M.A. With a Map and Notes. 8vo. 10s. 6d.

The Agricola and Germany.
By the same Translators. With Map and Notes. Fcap. 8vo. 2s. 6d.

TAIT AND STEELE.—*A Treatise on Dynamics.*
With numerous Examples. By P. G. TAIT and W. J. STEELE. Second Edition. Crown 8vo. 10s. 6d.

TAYLOR.—*Words and Places;*
Or, Etymological Illustrations of History, Ethnology, and Geography. By the Rev. ISAAC TAYLOR. Second Edition. Crown 8vo. 12s. 6d.

TAYLOR.—*The Restoration of Belief.*
New and Revised Edition. By ISAAC TAYLOR, Esq. Crown 8vo. 8s. 6d.

TAYLOR (C.).—*Geometrical Conics.*
By C. TAYLOR, B.A. Crown 8vo. 7s. 6d.

TEBAY.—*Elementary Mensuration for Schools,*
With numerous Examples. By SEPTIMUS TEBAY, B.A. Head Master of Queen Elizabeth's Grammar School, Rivington. Extra fcap. 8vo. 3s. 6d.

TEMPLE.—*Sermons preached in the Chapel of Rugby School.*
By F. TEMPLE, D.D. Head Master. *New and Cheaper Edition.* Crown 8vo. 7s. 6d.

THORPE.—*Diplomatarium Anglicum Ævi Saxonici.*
A Collection of English Charters, from the Reign of King Æthelberht of Kent, A.D. DC.V. to that of William the Conqueror. With a Translation of the Anglo-Saxon. By BENJAMIN THORPE, Member of the Royal Academy of Sciences, Munich. 8vo. cloth. 21s.

THRING.— *Works by* EDWARD THRING, M.A. *Head Master of Uppingham.*

A Construing Book.
Fcap. 8vo. 2s. 6d.

A Latin Gradual.
A First Latin Construing Book for Beginners. 18mo. 2s. 6d.

The Elements of Grammar taught in English.
Fourth Edition. 18mo. 2s.

THRING.—*The Child's Grammar.*
  A New Edition. 18mo. 1s.

  Sermons delivered at Uppingham School.
  Crown 8vo. 5s.

  School Songs.
  With the Music arranged for Four Voices. Edited by the Rev. EDWARD THRING, M.A. and H. RICCIUS. Small folio. 7s. 6d.

  Education and School.
  Second Edition. Crown 8vo. 6s.

  A Manual of Mood Constructions.
  Extra fcap. 8vo. 1s. 6d.

THRUPP.—*Works by the Rev.* J. F. THRUPP.

  The Song of Songs.
  A New Translation, with a Commentary and an Introduction. Crown 8vo. 7s. 6d.

  Introduction to the Study and Use of the Psalms.
  Two Vols. 8vo. 21s.

  Psalms and Hymns for Public Worship.
  Selected and Edited by the Rev. J. F. THRUPP, M.A. 18mo. 2s. Common paper, 1s. 4d.

  The Burden of Human Sin as borne by Christ.
  Three Sermons preached before the University of Cambridge in Lent, 1865. Crown 8vo. 3s. 6d.

THUCYDIDES.—*The Sicilian Expedition:*
  Being Books VI. and VII. of Thucydides, with Notes. By the Rev. PERCIVAL FROST, M.A. Fcap. 8vo. 5s.

TOCQUEVILLE.—*Memoir, Letters, and Remains of Alexis de Tocqueville.*
  Translated from the French by the Translator of "Napoleon's Correspondence with King Joseph." With numerous Additions. Two vols. Crown 8vo. 21s.

TODD.—*The Books of the Vaudois.*
  The Waldensian Manuscripts preserved in the Library of Trinity College, Dublin, with an Appendix by JAMES HENTHORN TODD, D.D. Crown 8vo. cloth. 6s.

TODHUNTER.—*Works by* ISAAC TODHUNTER, M.A. F.R.S.

Euclid for Colleges and Schools.
New Edition. 18mo. 3s. 6d.

Algebra for Beginners.
With numerous Examples. New Edition. 18mo. 2s. 6d.

Key to Algebra for Beginners.
Crown 8vo. 6s. 6d.

Mechanics for Beginners.
With numerous Examples. 18mo. 4s. 6d.

Trigonometry for Beginners.
With numerous Examples. 18mo. 2s. 6d.

A Treatise on the Differential Calculus.
With numerous Examples. Fourth Edition. Crown 8vo. 10s. 6d.

A Treatise on the Integral Calculus.
With numerous Examples. Third Edition. Crown 8vo. 10s. 6d.

A Treatise on Analytical Statics.
Third Edition. Crown 8vo. 10s. 6d.

A Treatise on Conic Sections.
Fourth Edition. Crown 8vo. 7s. 6d.

Algebra for the Use of Colleges and Schools.
Fourth Edition. Crown 8vo. 7s. 6d.

Plane Trigonometry for Colleges and Schools.
Third Edition. Crown 8vo. 5s.

A Treatise on Spherical Trigonometry for the Use of Colleges and Schools.
Second Edition. Crown 8vo. 4s. 6d.

Critical History of the Progress of the Calculus of Variations during the Nineteenth Century.
8vo. 12s.

Examples of Analytical Geometry of Three Dimensions.
Second Edition. Crown 8vo. 4s.

A Treatise on the Theory of Equations.
Second Edition. Crown 8vo. 7s. 6d.

Mathematical Theory of Probability.
8vo. 18s.

Tom Brown's School Days.
>By an OLD BOY. Fcap. 8vo. 5s.
>Golden Treasury Edition, 4s. 6d.
>PEOPLE'S EDITION, 2s.
>Illustrated Edition.

Tom Brown at Oxford.
>By the Author of "Tom Brown's School Days." *New Edition.* Crown 8vo. 6s.

Tracts for Priests and People. (*By various Writers.*)
>THE FIRST SERIES, Crown 8vo. 8s.
>THE SECOND SERIES, Crown 8vo. 8s.
>The whole Series of Fifteen Tracts may be had separately, price One Shilling each.

TRENCH.—*Works by* R. CHENEVIX TRENCH, D.D. *Archbishop of Dublin.*

>*Notes on the Parables of Our Lord.*
>>Tenth Edition. 8vo. 12s.
>
>*Notes on the Miracles of Our Lord.*
>>Eighth Edition. 8vo. 12s.
>
>*Synonyms of the New Testament.*
>>New Edition. One vol. 8vo. cloth. 10s. 6d.
>
>*On the Study of Words.*
>>Twelfth Edition. Fcap. 8vo. 4s.
>
>*English Past and Present.*
>>Sixth Edition. Fcap. 8vo. 4s. 6d.
>
>*Proverbs and their Lessons.*
>>Fifth Edition. Fcap. 8vo. 3s.
>
>*Select Glossary of English Words used formerly in Senses different from the present.*
>>Third Edition. Fcap. 8vo. 4s.
>
>*On some Deficiencies in our English Dictionaries.*
>>Second Edition. 8vo. 3s.
>
>*Sermons preached in Westminster Abbey.*
>>Second Edition. 8vo. 10s. 6d.
>
>*The Fitness of Holy Scripture for Unfolding the Spiritual Life of Man:*
>>Christ the Desire of all Nations; or, the Unconscious Prophecies of Heathendom. Hulsean Lectures. Fcap. 8vo. *Fourth Edition.* 5s.

TRENCH (R. CHENEVIX).—*On the Authorized Version of the New Testament.*
    Second Edition. 8vo. 7s.

Justin Martyr, and other Poems.
    Fifth Edition. Fcap. 8vo. 6s.

Gustavus Adolphus.—Social Aspects of the Thirty Years' War.
    Fcap. 8vo. 2s. 6d.

Poems.
    Collected and arranged anew. Fcap. 8vo. 7s. 6d.

Poems from Eastern Sources, Genoveva, and other Poems.
    Second Edition. Fcap. 8vo. 5s. 6d.

Elegiac Poems.
    Third Edition. Fcap. 8vo. 2s. 6d.

Calderon's Life's a Dream:
    The Great Theatre of the World. With an Essay on his Life and Genius. Fcap. 8vo. 4s. 6d.

Remains of the late Mrs. Richard Trench.
    Being Selections from her Journals, Letters, and other Papers. New and Cheaper Issue. With Portrait. 8vo. 6s.

Commentary on the Epistles to the Seven Churches in Asia.
    Third Edition, revised. 8vo. 8s. 6d.

Sacred Latin Poetry.
    Chiefly Lyrical. Selected and arranged for Use. Second Edition. Corrected and Improved. Fcap. 8vo. 7s.

Studies in the Gospels.
    Second Edition. 8vo. 10s. 6d.

Shipwrecks of Faith:
    Three Sermons preached before the University of Cambridge in May, 1867. Fcap. 8vo. 2s. 6d.

A Household Book of English Poetry.
    Selected and Arranged with Notes. By the ARCHBISHOP OF DUBLIN. Extra fcap. 8vo. 5s. 6d.

TRENCH (REV. FRANCIS).—*Brief Notes on the Greek of the New Testament (for English Readers).*
    Crown 8vo. cloth. 6s.

TREVELYAN.—*Works by* G. O. TREVELYAN, M.P.

The Competition Wallah.
New Edition. Crown 8vo. 6s.

Cawnpore,
Illustrated with Plan. Second Edition. Crown 8vo. 6s.

TUDOR—*The Decalogue viewed as the Christian's Law.*
With Special Reference to the Questions and Wants of the Times.
By the Rev. RICH. TUDOR, B.A. Crown 8vo. 10s. 6d.

TULLOCH.—*The Christ of the Gospels and the Christ of Modern Criticism.*
Lectures on M. RENAN's "Vie de Jésus." By JOHN TULLOCH, D.D. Principal of the College of St. Mary, in the University of St. Andrew. Extra fcap. 8vo. 4s. 6d.

TURNER.—*Sonnets.*
By the Rev. CHARLES TENNYSON TURNER. Dedicated to his Brother, the Poet Laureate. Fcap. 8vo. 4s. 6d.

Small Tableaux.
By the Rev. C. TURNER. Fcap. 8vo. 4s. 6d.

TYRWHITT.—*The Schooling of Life.*
By R. ST. JOHN TYRWHITT, M.A. Vicar of St. Mary Magdalen, Oxford. Fcap. 8vo. 3s. 6d.

Vacation Tourists;
And Notes of Travel in 1861. Edited by F. GALTON, F.R.S.
With Ten Maps illustrating the Routes. 8vo. 14s.

Vacation Tourists;
And Notes of Travel in 1862 and 1863. Edited by FRANCIS GALTON, F.R.S. 8vo. 16s.

VAUGHAN.—*Works by* CHARLES J. VAUGHAN, D.D. *Vicar of Doncaster.*

Notes for Lectures on Confirmation.
With suitable Prayers. Sixth Edition. Fcap. 8vo. 1s. 6d.

Lectures on the Epistle to the Philippians.
Second Edition. Crown 8vo. 7s. 6d.

Lectures on the Revelation of St. John.
Second Edition. Two vols. crown 8vo. 15s.

VAUGHAN (CHARLES J.).—**Epiphany, Lent, and Easter.**
A Selection of Expository Sermons. *Third Edition.* Crown 8vo. 10s. 6d.

The Book and the Life,
And other Sermons, preached before the University of Cambridge. *New Edition.* Fcap. 8vo. 4s. 6d.

Memorials of Harrow Sundays.
A Selection of Sermons preached in Harrow School Chapel. With a View of the Chapel. *Fourth Edition.* Crown 8vo. 10s. 6d.

St. Paul's Epistle to the Romans.
The Greek Text with English Notes. Crown 8vo. 5s. *New Edition in the Press.*

Twelve Discourses on Subjects connected with the Liturgy and Worship of the Church of England.
Fcap. 8vo. 6s.

Lessons of Life and Godliness.
A Selection of Sermons preached in the Parish Church of Doncaster. *Third Edition.* Fcap. 8vo. 4s. 6d.

Words from the Gospels.
A Second Selection of Sermons preached in the Parish Church of Doncaster. *Second Edition.* Fcap. 8vo. 4s. 6d.

The Epistles of St. Paul.
For English Readers. Part I. containing the First Epistle to the Thessalonians. *Second Edition.* 8vo. 1s. 6d. Each Epistle will be published separately.

The Church of the First Days.
Series I. The Church of Jerusalem. *Second Edition.*
  ,, II. The Church of the Gentiles. *Second Edition.*
  ,, III. The Church of the World. *Second Edition.*
Fcap. 8vo. cloth. 4s. 6d. each.

Life's Work and God's Discipline.
Three Sermons. Fcap. 8vo. cloth. 2s. 6d.

The Wholesome Words of Jesus Christ.
Four Sermons preached before the University of Cambridge in November, 1866. Fcap. 8vo. cloth. 3s. 6d. *New Edition in the Press.*

Foes of Faith.
Sermons preached before the University of Cambridge in November, 1868.

VAUGHAN.—*Works by* DAVID J. VAUGHAN, M.A. *Vicar of St. Martin's, Leicester.*

Sermons preached in St. John's Church, Leicester,
During the Years 1855 and 1856. Crown 8vo. 5s. 6d.

Sermons on the Resurrection.
With a Preface. Fcap. 8vo. 3s.

Three Sermons on the Atonement.
1s. 6d.

Sermons on Sacrifice and Propitiation.
2s. 6d.

Christian Evidences and the Bible.
New Edition. Revised and enlarged. Fcap. 8vo. cloth. 5s. 6d.

VAUGHAN.—*Memoir of Robert A. Vaughan,*
Author of "Hours with the Mystics." By ROBERT VAUGHAN, D.D. Second Edition. Revised and enlarged. Extra fcap. 8vo. 5s.

VENN.—*The Logic of Chance.*
An Essay on the Foundations and Province of the Theory of Probability, with special reference to its application to Moral and Social Science. By the Rev. J. VENN, M.A. Fcap. 8vo. 7s. 6d.

Village Sermons.
By a NORTHAMPTONSHIRE RECTOR. With a Preface on the Inspiration of Holy Scripture. Crown 8vo. 6s.

Vittoria Colonna.—Life and Poems.
By MRS. HENRY ROSCOE. Crown 8vo. 9s.

Volunteer's Scrap Book.
By the Author of "The Cambridge Scrap Book." Crown 4to. 7s. 6d.

WAGNER.—*Memoir of the Rev. George Wagner,*
late of St. Stephen's, Brighton. By J. N. SIMPKINSON, M.A. Third and Cheaper Edition. 5s.

WALLACE.—*The Malay Archipelago : The Home of the Orang Utan and the Bird of Paradise.*
A Narrative of Travel. With Studies of Man and Nature. By ALFRED RUSSEL WALLACE. With Maps and Illustrations.

WARREN.—*An Essay on Greek Federal Coinage.*
  By the Hon. J. LEICESTER WARREN, M.A. 8vo. 2s. 6d.

WEBSTER.—*Works by* AUGUSTA WEBSTER.

Dramatic Studies.
  Extra fcap. 8vo. 5s.

A Woman Sold,
  And other Poems. Crown 8vo. 7s. 6d.

Prometheus Bound, of Æschylus,
  Literally Translated into English Verse. Extra fcap. 8vo. 3s. 6d.

Medea of Euripides,
  Literally Translated into English Verse. Extra fcap. 8vo. 3s. 6d.

WESTCOTT.—*Works by* BROOKE FOSS WESTCOTT, B.D. *Examining Chaplain to the Bishop of Peterborough.*

A General Survey of the History of the Canon of the New Testament during the First Four Centuries.
  Second Edition, revised. Crown 8vo. 10s. 6d.

Characteristics of the Gospel Miracles.
  Sermons preached before the University of Cambridge. *With Notes.* Crown 8vo. 4s. 6d.

Introduction to the Study of the Four Gospels.
  Third Edition. Crown 8vo. 10s. 6d.

The Gospel of the Resurrection.
  Thoughts on its Relation to Reason and History. *New Edition.* Fcap. 8vo. 4s. 6d.

The Bible in the Church.
  A Popular Account of the Collection and Reception of the Holy Scriptures in the Christian Churches. *Second Edition.* 18mo. 4s. 6d.

History of the English Bible.
  Crown 8vo. 10s. 6d.

Westminster Plays.
  Lusus Alteri Westmonasterienses, Sive Prologi et Epilogi ad Fabulas in S^{ti} Petri Collegio: actas qui Exstabant collecti et justa quoad licuit annorum serie ordinati, quibus accedit Declamationum quæ vocantur et Epigrammatum Delectus. Curantibus J. MURE, A.M., H. BULL, A.M., C. B. SCOTT, B.D. 8vo. 12s. 6d.
  IDEM.—Pars Secunda, 1820—1865. Quibus accedit Epigrammatum Delectus. 8vo. 15s.

WILSON.—*Works by* GEORGE WILSON, M.D.
  Counsels of an Invalid.
    Letters on Religious Subjects. With Vignette Portrait. Fcap. 8vo. 4s. 6d.

  Religio Chemici.
    With a Vignette beautifully engraved after a Design by Sir NOEL PATON. Crown 8vo. 8s. 6d.

WILSON (GEORGE).—*The Five Gateways of Knowledge.*
    New Edition. Fcap. 8vo. 2s. 6d. Or in Paper Covers, 1s.

  The Progress of the Telegraph.
    Fcap. 8vo. 1s.

WILSON.—*An English, Hebrew, and Chaldee Lexicon and Concordance.*
    By WILLIAM WILSON, D.D. Canon of Winchester. Second Edition. 4to. 25s.

WILSON.—*Memoir of George Wilson,* M.D. F.R.S.E.
    Regius Professor of Technology in the University of Edinburgh. By HIS SISTER. New Edition. Crown 8vo. 6s.

WILSON.—*Works by* DANIEL WILSON, LL.D.
  Prehistoric Annals of Scotland.
    New Edition. With numerous Illustrations. Two Vols. demy 8vo. 36s.

  Prehistoric Man.
    New Edition. Revised and partly re-written, with numerous Illustrations. One vol. 8vo. 21s.

WILSON.—*A Treatise on Dynamics.*
    By W. P. WILSON, M.A. 8vo. 9s. 6d.

WILSON.—*Elementary Geometry.*
    PART I.—Angles, Triangles, Parallels, and Equivalent Figures, with the application to Problems. By J. M. WILSON, M.A. Fellow of St. John's College, Cambridge, and Mathematical Master at Rugby. Extra fcap. 8vo. 2s. 6d.

WINSLOW.—*Force and Nature. Attraction and Repulsion.*
    The Radical Principles of Energy graphically discussed in their Relations to Physical and Morphological Development. By C. F. WINSLOW, M.D. 8vo. [In the press.

WOLLASTON.—*Lyra Devoniensis.*
> By T. V. WOLLASTON, M.A. Fcap. 8vo. 3s. 6d.

WOLSTENHOLME.—*A Book of Mathematical Problems.*
> Crown 8vo. 8s. 6d.

WOODFORD.—*Christian Sanctity.*
> By JAMES RUSSELL WOODFORD, M.A. Fcap. 8vo. cloth. 3s.

WOODWARD.—*Works by the Rev.* HENRY WOODWARD, *edited by his Son,* THOMAS WOODWARD, M.A. *Dean of Down.*

> *Essays, Thoughts and Reflections, and Letters.*
> Fifth Edition. Crown 8vo. 10s. 6d.

> *The Shunammite.*
> Second Edition. Crown 8vo. 10s. 6d.

> *Sermons.*
> Fifth Edition. Crown 8vo. 10s. 6d.

WOOLLEY.—*Lectures delivered in Australia.*
> By the late JOHN WOOLLEY, D.C.L. Crown 8vo. 8s. 6d.

WOOLNER.—*My Beautiful Lady.*
> By THOMAS WOOLNER. With a Vignette by ARTHUR HUGHES. Third Edition. Fcap. 8vo. 5s.

Words from the Poets.
> Selected by the Editor of "Rays of Sunlight." With a Vignette and Frontispiece. 18mo. Extra cloth gilt. 2s. 6d. Cheaper Edition, 18mo. limp. 1s.

Worship (The) of God and Fellowship among Men.
> Sermons on Public Worship. By PROFESSOR MAURICE, and Others. Fcap. 8vo. 3s. 6d.

WORSLEY.—*Christian Drift of Cambridge Work.*
> Eight Lectures. By T. WORSLEY, D.D. Master of Downing College, Cambridge. Crown 8vo. cloth. 6s.

WRIGHT.—*Works by* J. WRIGHT, M.A.

> *Hellenica;*
> Or, a History of Greece in Greek, as related by Diodorus and Thucydides, being a First Greek Reading Book, with Explanatory Notes Critical and Historical. Third Edition. WITH A VOCABULARY. 12mo. 3s. 6d.

The Seven Kings of Rome.
An Easy Narrative, abridged from the First Book of Livy by the omission of difficult passages, being a First Latin Reading Book, with Grammatical Notes. Fcap. 8vo. 3s.

A Vocabulary and Exercises on the "Seven Kings of Rome."
Fcap. 8vo. 2s. 6d.
*** The Vocabulary and Exercises may also be had bound up with "The Seven Kings of Rome." Price 5s.

A Help to Latin Grammar;
Or, the Form and Use of Words in Latin, with Progressive Exercises. Crown 8vo. 4s. 6d.

David, King of Israel.
Readings for the Young. With Six Illustrations. Royal 16mo. cloth, gilt. 3s. 6d.

YOUMANS.—*Modern Culture,*
Its True Aims and Requirements. A Series of Addresses and Arguments on the Claims of Scientific Education. Edited by EDWARD L. YOUMANS, M.D. Crown 8vo. 8s. 6d.

Works by the Author of
"THE HEIR OF REDCLYFFE."

The Prince and the Page. A Book for the Young. 16mo. 3s. 6d.

A Book of Golden Deeds. 18mo. 4s. 6d. Cheap Edition, 1s.

History of Christian Names. Two. Vols. Crown 8vo. 1l. 1s.

The Heir of Redclyffe. Seventeenth Edition. With Illustrations. Crown 8vo. 6s.

Dynevor Terrace. Third Edition. Crown 8vo. 6s.

The Daisy Chain. Ninth Edition. With Illustrations. Crown 8vo. 6s.

The Trial: More Links of the Daisy Chain. Fourth Edition. With Illustrations. Crown 8vo. 6s.

Heartsease. Tenth Edition. With Illustrations. Crown 8vo. 6s.

Hopes and Fears. Third Edition. Crown 8vo. 6s.

The Young Stepmother. Second Edition. Crown 8vo. 6s.

The Lances of Lynwood. With Coloured Illustrations. Second Edition. Extra fcap. cloth. 4s. 6d.

The Little Duke. New Edition. 18mo. cloth. 3s. 6d.

Clever Woman of the Family. Crown 8vo. 6s.

Danvers Papers; an Invention. Crown 8vo. 4s. 6d.

Dove in the Eagle's Nest. Two vols. Crown 8vo. 12s.

Cameos from English History. From Rollo to Edward II. Extra fcap. 8vo. 5s.

Book of Worthies. [In the Press.

ELEMENTARY SCHOOL CLASS BOOKS.

The Volumes of this Series of ELEMENTARY SCHOOL CLASS BOOKS *are handsomely printed in a form that, it is hoped, will assist the young Student as much as clearness of type and distinctness of arrangement can effect. They are published at a moderate price, to insure an extensive sale in the Schools of the United Kingdom and the Colonies.*

Euclid for Colleges and Schools.
By I. TODHUNTER, M.A. F.R.S. 18mo. 3s. 6d.

Algebra for Beginners.
By I. TODHUNTER, M.A. F.R.S. 18mo. 2s. 6d.

Key to Algebra for Beginners.
Crown 8vo. 6s. 6d.

The School Class Book of Arithmetic.
By BARNARD SMITH, M.A. Parts I. and II. 18mo. limp cloth, price 10d. each. Part III. 1s.; or Three Parts in one Volume, price 3s.
KEY TO CLASS BOOK OF ARITHMETIC.
Complete, 18mo. cloth, price 6s. 6d. Or separately, Parts I. II. & III. 2s. 6d. each.

Mythology for Latin Versification.
A Brief Sketch of the Fables of the Ancients, prepared to be rendered into Latin Verse for Schools. By F. HODGSON, B.D. *New Edition.* Revised by F. C. HODGSON, M.A. Fellow of King's College, Cambridge. 18mo. 3s.

A Latin Gradual for Beginners.
A First Latin Construing Book. By EDWARD THRING, M.A. 18mo. 2s. 6d.

Shakespeare's Tempest.
The Text taken from "The Cambridge Shakespeare." With Glossarial and Explanatory Notes. By the Rev. J. M. JEPHSON. 18mo. cloth limp. 1s. 6d.

Lessons in Elementary Botany.
The Part on Systematic Botany based upon Material left in Manuscript by the late Professor HENSLOW. With nearly Two Hundred Illustrations. By DANIEL OLIVER, F.R.S. F.L.S. 18mo. cloth. 4s. 6d.

Lessons in Elementary Physiology.
With numerous Illustrations. By T. H. HUXLEY, F.R.S. Professor of Natural History in the Government School of Mines. 18mo. 4s. 6d.

Popular Astronomy.
A Series of Lectures delivered at Ipswich. By GEORGE BIDDELL AIRY, Astronomer Royal. 18mo. cloth. 4s. 6d.

Lessons in Elementary Chemistry.
By HENRY ROSCOE, F.R.S. Professor of Chemistry in Owens College, Manchester. With numerous Illustrations. 18mo. cloth. 4s. 6d.

An Elementary History of the Book of Common Prayer.
By FRANCIS PROCTER, M.A. 18mo. 2s. 6d.

Algebraical Exercises.
Progressively arranged by Rev. C. A. JONES, M.A. and C. H. CHEYNE, M.A. Mathematical Masters in Westminster School. 18mo. cloth. 2s. 6d.

The Bible in the Church.
A Popular Account of the Collection and Reception of the Holy Scriptures in the Christian Churches. By BROOKE FOSS WESTCOTT, B.D. 18mo. 4s. 6d.

The Bible Word Book.
A Glossary of Old English Bible Words. By J. EASTWOOD, M.A. and W ALDIS WRIGHT, M.A. 18mo. 5s. 6d.

MACMILLAN AND CO. LONDON.

www.ingramcontent.com/pod-product-compliance
Lightning Source LLC
Chambersburg PA
CBHW030250170426
43202CB00009B/687